Samsung S21 user guide

A step by step illustrated guide to help you get the most from your S21
2021

Bernard Gates

Copyright@2021

Introduction

The new Samsung S21 made its official debut on January 14 this year and its already on sale. It is a fully 5G device and retails from $799. It replaces the S20 and it's cheaper to buy than the phone its replacing. The S21 is the least in the S21 lineup but it still performs great. Here's a look at the specs: it weighs 169g, it has a 6.2-inch HD + AMOLED display and a resolution of 2400x1080. The refresh rate is 120Hz and it has a pixel density of 421 ppi. Versions sold in the US comes with the snapdragon 888 while versions sold elsewhere are fitted with the Exynos 2100 chipset. An 8GB RAM and buyers can choose between 128GB and 256GB of storage space

The S21 sports rear cameras of 12MP+64MP+12MP and a front camera of 10MP. Samsung has termed the camera its Contour Cut camera. The battery is a 4000 MAh affair and it can last up to a day on a single charge. The rear of the S21 is made of a material that's half glass and half plastic so it's called Glasstic.

On the downside, there is no microSD support, so buyers would have to make do with the internally available storage. Similarly, there is no charger included as part of the package. There is a sim tray and a USB-C port but the Bixby button and the 3.5mm audio jack are not included.

The S21 has an improved fingerprint scanner over the S20 and Samsung has made software tweaks to the camera such as adding a director's view, vlogger's view and the ability to take 8K stills from 8K video. Also, there is now a slo-mo setting for the Single Take camera feature.

There are four color choices for buyers: phantom white, phantom pink, phantom violet and phantom gray.

Generally, the S21 is a solid and capable device that buyers would find a delight to use.

Chapter one: Set Up

Setting up your new Samsung S21

Congratulations!!! You just purchased your new S21. If you are new to the Samsung brand or you just upgraded to a better device, you would need to setup your new device in order to get it running. In case you are wondering how to proceed, fret not. Just follow the steps below:

- Make sure that the device is optimally charged
- Next, install your **SIM(s)**

- Turn on the device using the **side button or key** as shown above, push and hold until you feel a vibration and the Samsung Logo shows on the display
- Next, follow the prompts from the **set-up wizard** to do the first-time set-up of your S21. Use the **set-up wizard** to specify the following settings:
- **Language**. Use the drop-down menu to do so. Tap the blue arrow when you are done

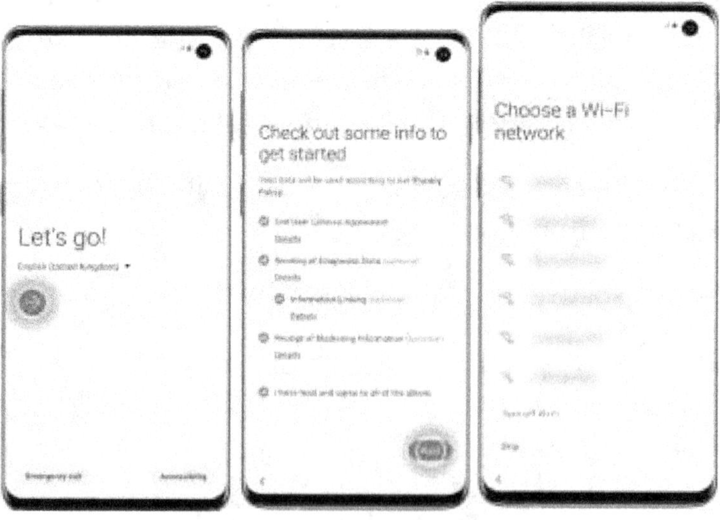

- Agree to the terms and conditions
- Connect to a Wi-Fi network. Choose a Wi-Fi, enter the password if required and tap Connect or tap **Skip** at bottom left of screen if you prefer to do that later
- Your device would now check for software updates and would automatically move to the next step when all updates are downloaded and installed. That's if you set a Wi-Fi connection. If you don't, this step won't happen
- The next step is to copy your apps and data from a previous or old device. you can use the Samsung Smart Switch to do this. Tap **Next** at bottom right of screen and follow the on-screen steps. If you prefer to do so later, tap **Don't copy** at bottom left

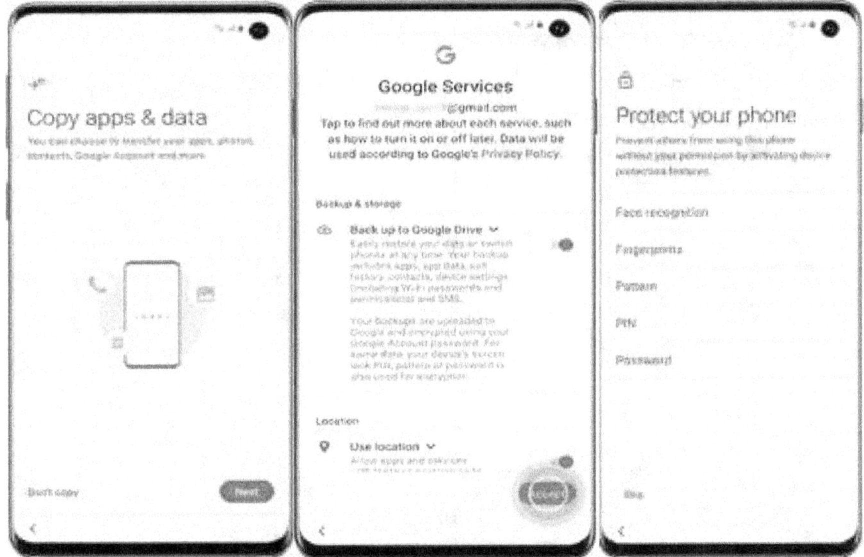

- After copying your apps and data from your old device, create or log in to your Google account. You can **Skip** or do it later
- Next, select Google services to enable, permit or activate and then tap **Accept** to continue
- Set up a protection method for your device or **Skip** it to do it later
- On the next screen, you would be asked to select Samsung apps to download. Do the select and tap **OK**

- Next, create or log into your **Samsung Account** or tap **Skip** to return to it later

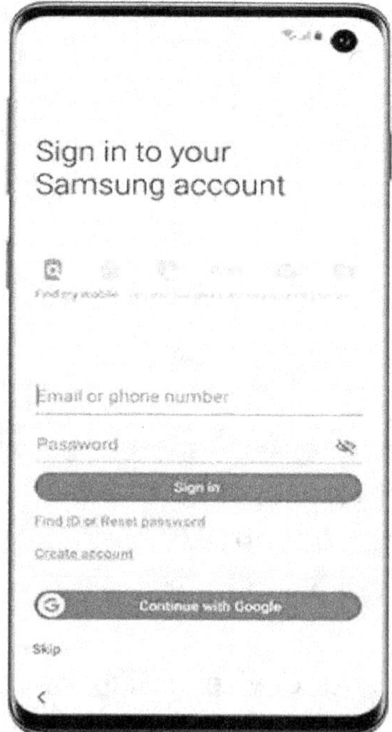

- Tap **Finish** to end or conclude the set-up
  You can now get proceed to get familiarized with your new S21.

Dual SIM settings

In case you inserted two SIMs into your phone, it's possible for you to specify particular settings as regards each SIM. For e.g, you can specify what SIM to use for sending messages, Data connection and making calls. You can when necessary, deactivate any of the SIMS. Follow the steps below to adjust your SIM settings:

- Launch the notifications panel by **swiping down** from screen top
- Tap the **Settings** symbol
- Select **Connections**
- Select **SIM card manager**

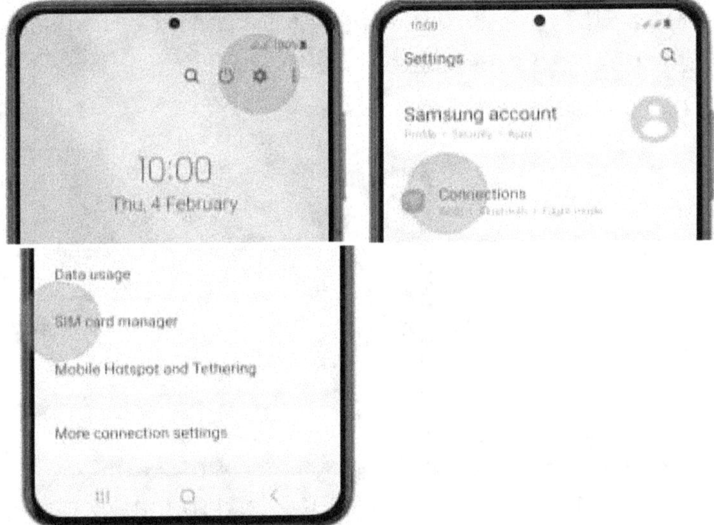

- To activate or deactivate a SIM, turn the indicator switch off or on

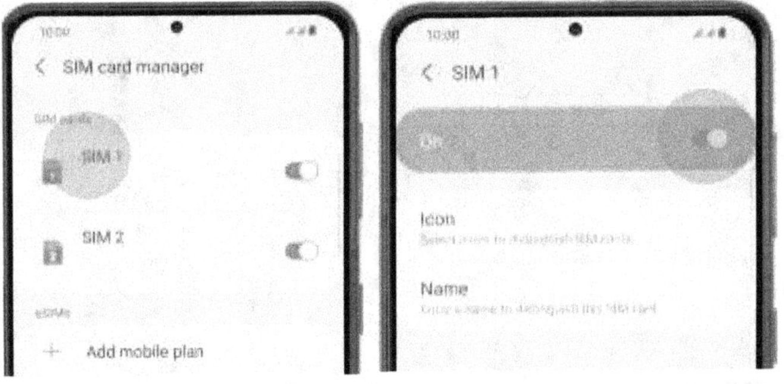

- To specify or choose a SIM for making calls, from the SIM card manager display, tap **calls**
- Specify the required setting

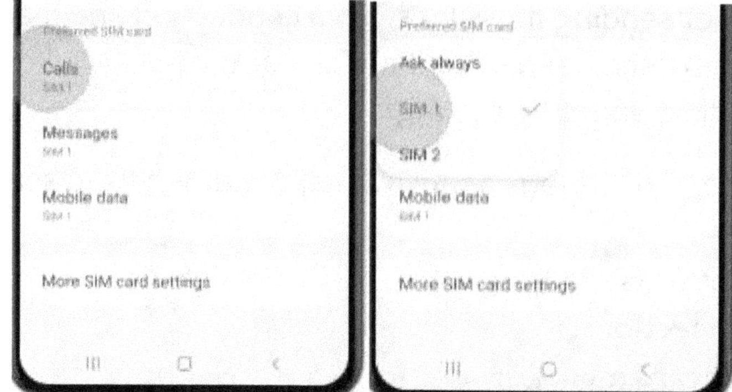

- To select a SIM for sending messages, from the SIM card manager page, tap **messages**
- Next, tap the **selected SIM**

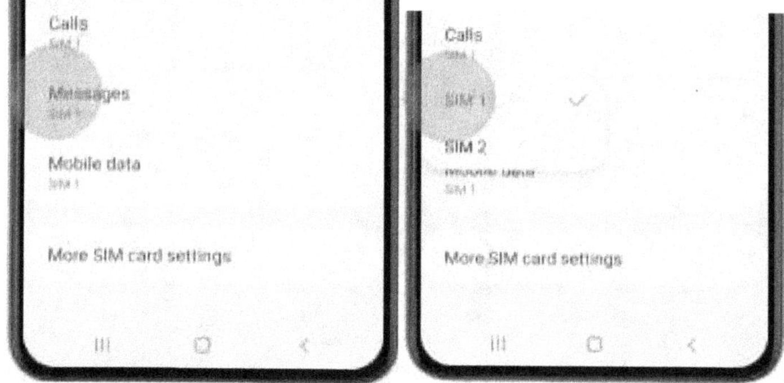

- For mobile data, from the same SIM card manager page, tap **Mobile data**
- Select required SIM card and return to home screen when done

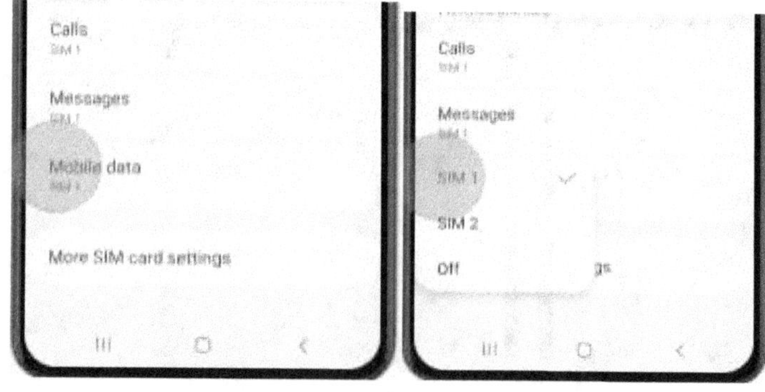

Chapter 2: Transferring Content

Transferring Data and Stuff from other Devices

If you didn't move your data and content from your previous device during the initial set-up, you can do it now. When it comes to moving data such as contacts, photos, mail, music, documents, messages, etc from a previous device, you have several options: you can transfer from iOS to android, you can do a cross- android transfer. For any of the options you prefer to use, find how to do so below:

Moving data from iOS to android

You do this via the smart switch app which is a Samsung designed app for moving content from iOS to Galaxy devices.

- The first step is to make sure that you have done a current sync or backup of your data to iCloud on your iOS device:
    1. Go to **Settings**
    2. Tap **Apple ID**
    3. Tap **iCloud backup**
    4. Enable or tap **Back up now**

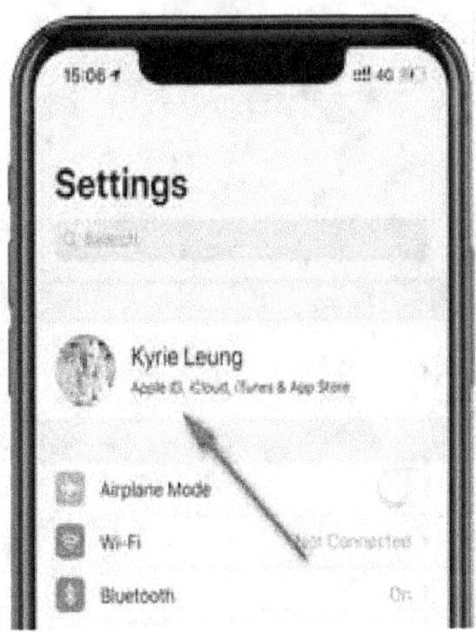

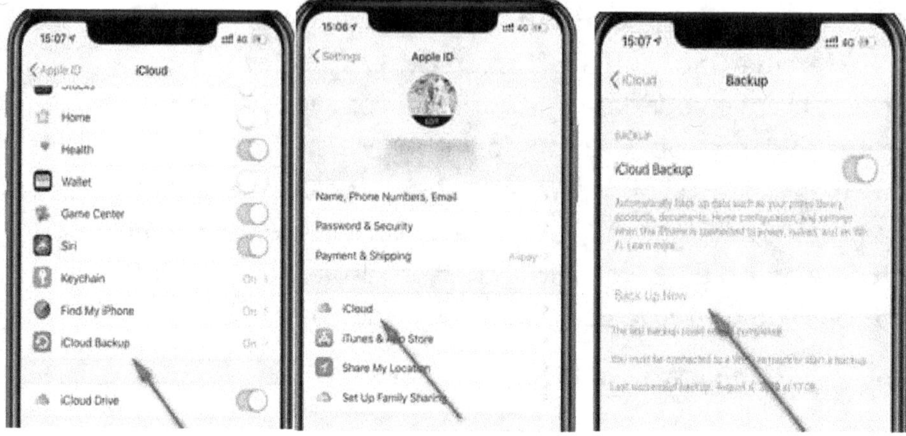

- Launch **smart switch** on your S21
- Select **wireless** to choose mode of content transfer
- Select **Receive** on the next screen
- Choose **iOS** from the list on the next display
- Sign in with your **Apple ID**
- Key in the **verification code** and tap **Ok**

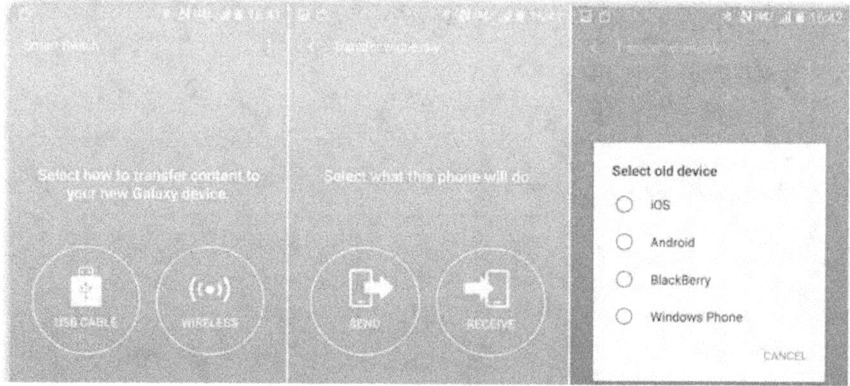

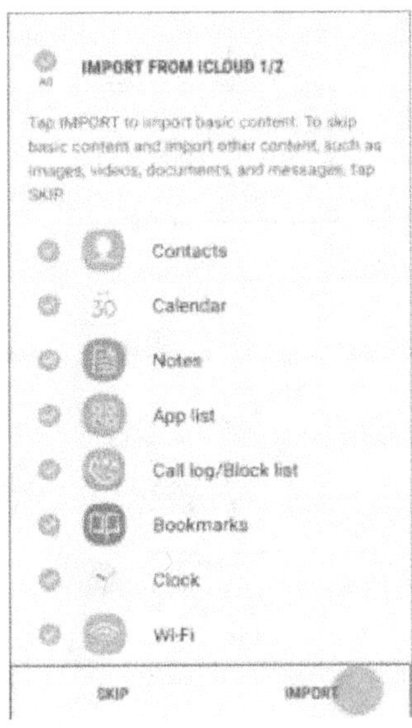

- From the content list on your iCloud data, tick the boxes of the content you want to transfer to your S21
- Enable the transfer by clicking **Import**

Transferring data from iPhone to your S21 via USB cable

- The first step is to attach the **USB OGT connector** that came with your device to your new phone
- Next, establish a connection between your old iPhone and the S21 via Lighting USB cable
- Tap **TRUST** on your iPhone when you view the pop-up message
- Tap **RECEIVE** when the smart switch app opens on your S21
- Tap ALLOW on your old iPhone when its required so you can move to the next step
- Next, choose all the content you want to move to your S21
- Finally, tap **TRANSFER**

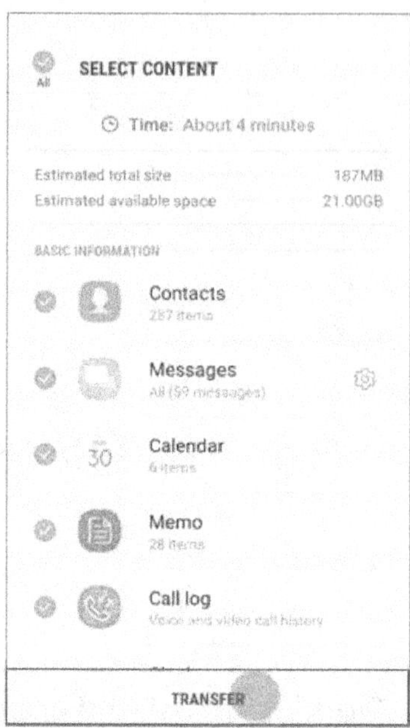

Transferring Data via Mac or PC from your old iPhone to your new S21

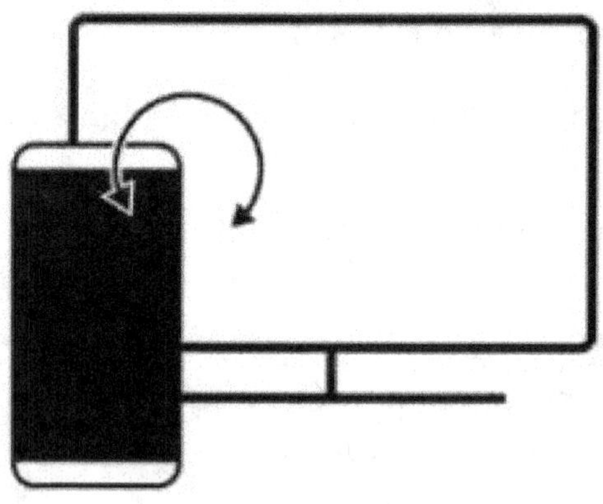

- Launch or go to **iTunes** on your Mac or from your PC
- Connect your iPhone to Mac or PC via the **Lightning** cable
- If prompted, select **Continue or Trust** to permit your Mac or PC to access the contents of your phone
- Next, select your iPhone name in iTunes
- Go to **Summary**

- Tap **Encrypt iPhone backup**
- Tap **This Computer**
- Tap **Back Up now**
- When done, disconnect your iPhone from Mac or PC by selecting the iTunes **eject icon** and removing the cable
- On your Mac or PC, make sure you have **Smart Switch** downloaded and installed. (If you don't have it, download it from iTunes or the Google Play store)
- Launch **Smart Switch** on your Mac or PC, connect your S21 and select **Restore** from the Smart Switch Menu
- Select **Restore Now,** tap **Select a Different Backup** and select **iTunes Backup Data** from top left of the Smart Switch menu
- Uncheck or deselect any content or data you are not interested in transferring and tap OK.
- Finally, tap **Restore Now** and **Allow.** You selected data or content would begin transferring

Transferring Data and content from an Android Device
To transfer content and data wirelessly, follow the steps below:

- make sure that you have **Samsung smart switch** installed on both devices
- Turn on both devices and launch the **Samsung Smart Switch** app on both phones
- Next, on your old device, tap **WIRELESS** in the Smart Switch app

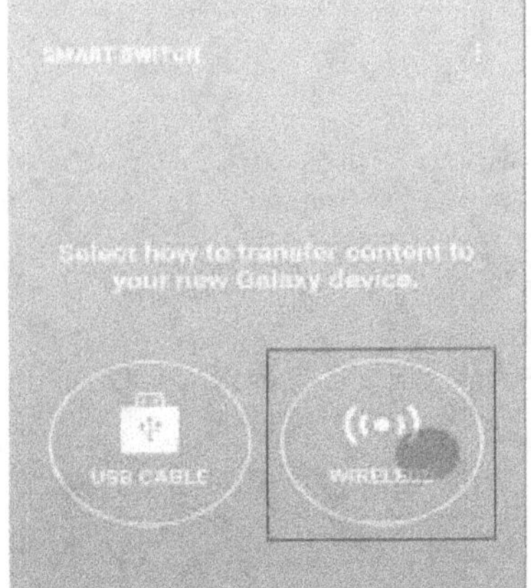

- Repeat last step as above on your new S21
- On the old device, tap **SEND** as shown below

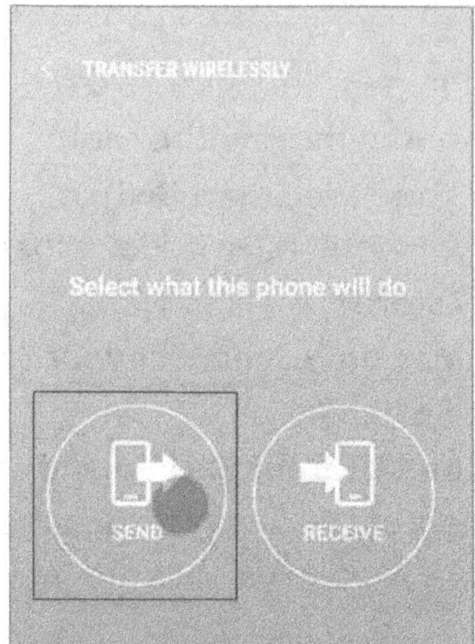

- On the S21, tap **RECEIVE**

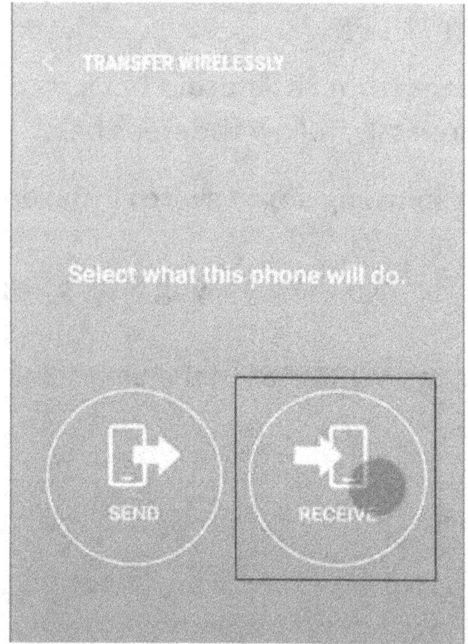

- From your old device, tap **CONNECT** at screen bottom
- On the S21, tap or select **Android**

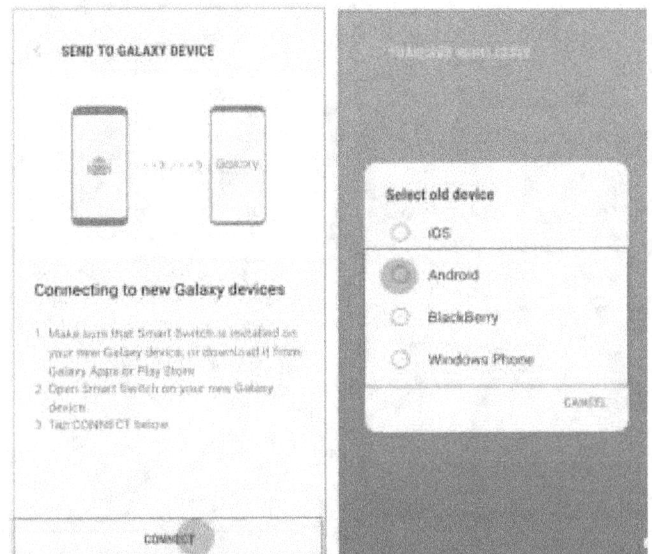

- From the old device, select the content to be moved to the S21. You can also deselect content you prefer not to move to the S21 and then tap **SEND** at screen bottom

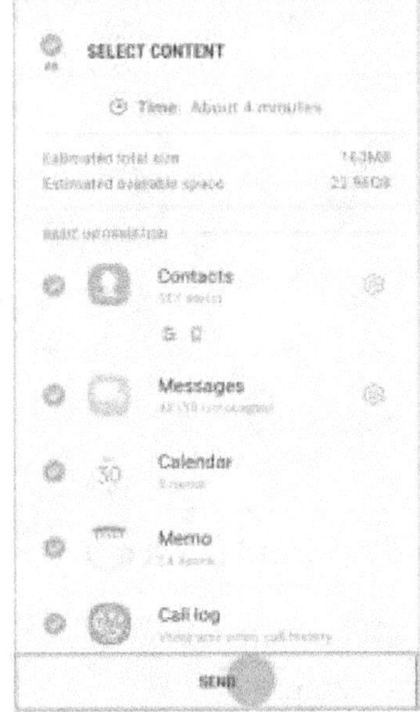

- Tap **RECEIVE** on your new phone

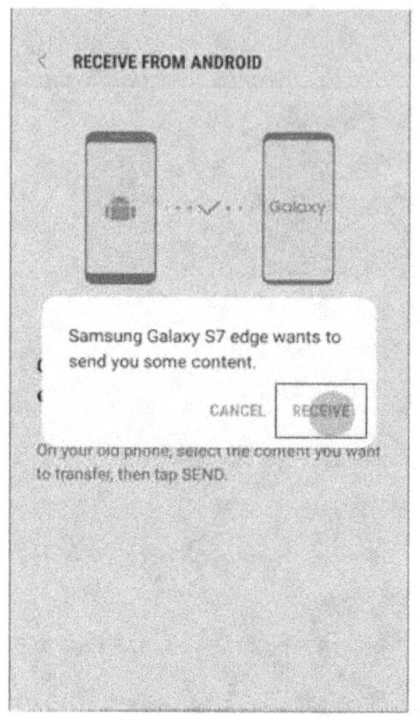

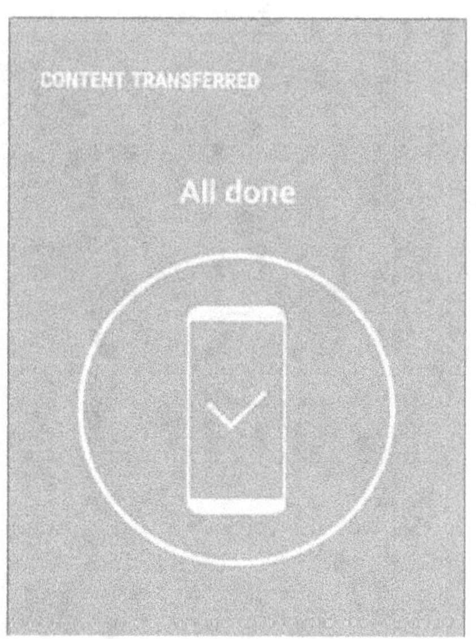

- When the transfer is done, on both devices, tap **CLOSE APP.** To access additional features on your new S21, after the transfer, tap **MORE FEATURES** at screen bottom

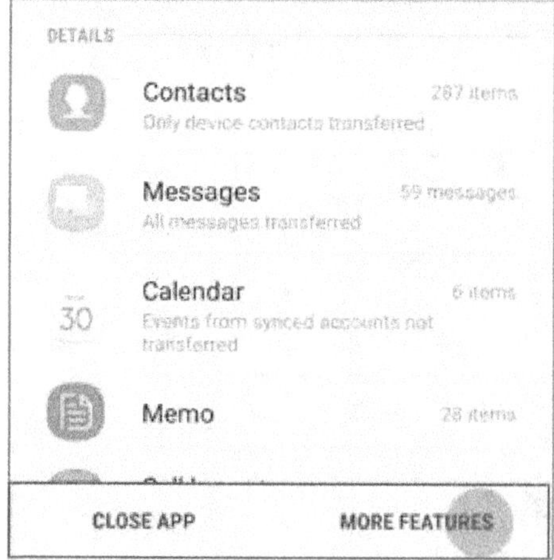

Transferring Data via USB Cable from old Android Device to S21

- Turn on both devices
- Connect a USB connector to your new S21
- Establish a connection between both devices using the USB cable you would use to charge your old device

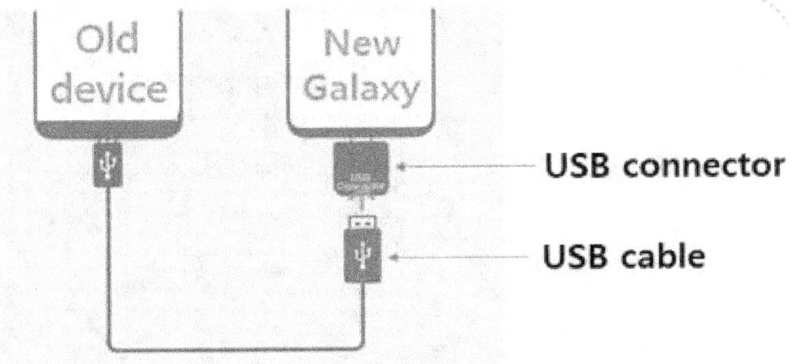

- When a connection between both devices is established, the Smart Switch app should launch automatically on your S21. Tap **RECEIVE**. Be prepared to manually launch the **Smart Switch** app and tap **USB CABLE** in case the auto launch doesn't happen

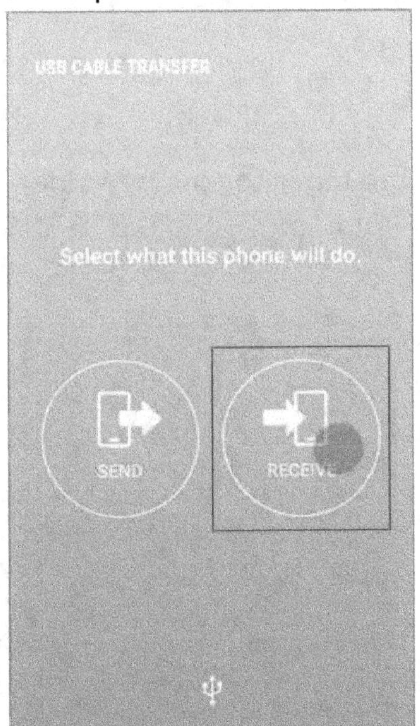

- Next, tap **ALLOW** on your old device to move to the next step
- Be patient as your S21 scans your old device for transferrable content

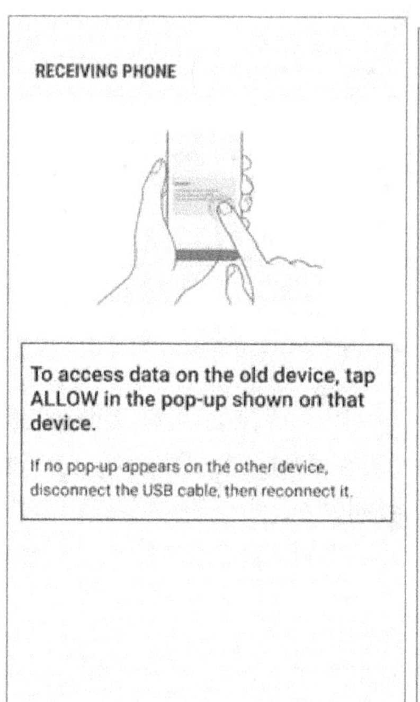

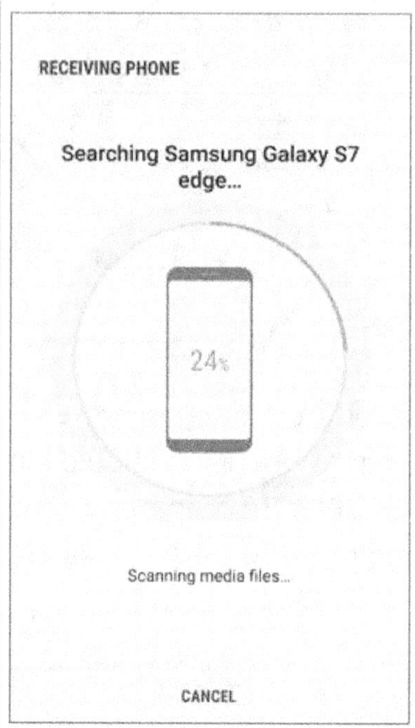

- Specify the content you want to move to your new phone and deselect the ones you prefer not to move and tap **TRANSFER**

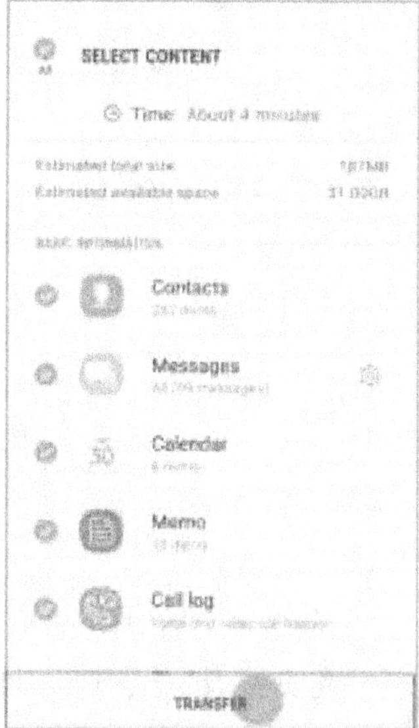

- Tap **CLOSE APP** to finish the process or tap **MORE FEATURES** at screen bottom if you prefer to view other options

Moving Data to your S21 via PC

- Download and install **Samsung Smart Switch** on your windows PC or Mac
- Establish a connection between your old device and your windows PC or Mac

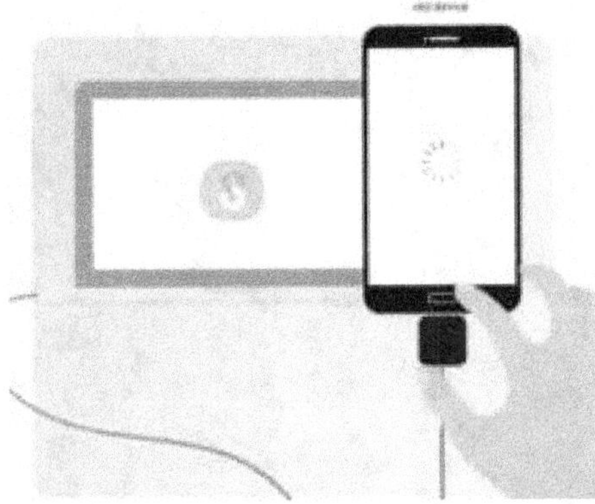

- Next, from the **Smart Switch menu interface,** tap **Backup**
- Tap **Allow** on your phone to begin the transfer
- When the backup process is done, click **OK** to end the process and disconnect the phone
- Next, connect your S21 to your Windows PC or Mac
- Select **Restore** from the Smart Switch menu interface
- Click **Select a different backup**
- Click **Samsung device data**

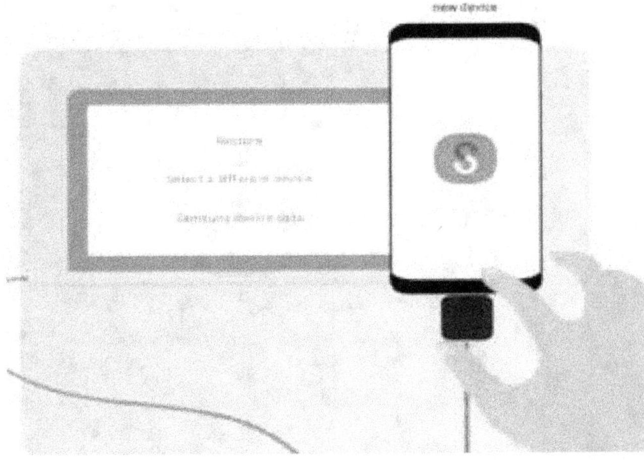

- Uncheck or deselect information you don't want to copy and click **OK**
- Click **Restore Now,** click **Allow**
- Your content or data should begin transferring

Chapter 3: Navigation, Familiarization and Customization

Using your new device is very simple, easy and uncomplicated. Samsung has taken great care to make sure that users quickly get used to their new S21 without much hassles. Even users making the switch from iOS to Android won't feel out of their depth. In this chapter, find the location of buttons and switches, how to use and customize your home screen, find and use apps, quick settings and more.

Buttons and peripherals

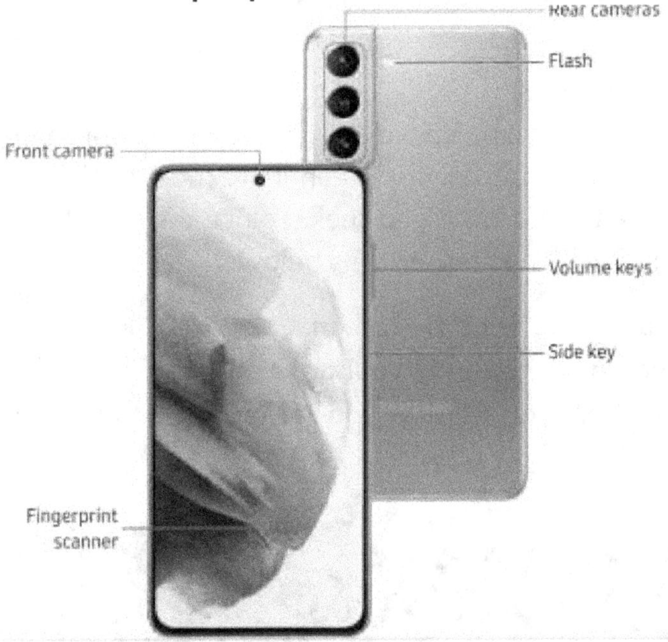

Finding and navigating between Apps screens

- To view the preinstalled apps, **swipe upwards** from your home screen.
- If you have a lot of apps on your device, **swipe left** to call up or view the next page of apps.
- To go back to the previous app screen, **swipe right.**
- To launch an app, just **tap on it.**
- To view more options about an app, **tap and hold it.**

Using the Search Function

You can use this function to locate specific settings, email contents, files etc. using this function enables you to eliminate most of the steps you would normally use to find what you seek. To use the search function to locate anything, follow the steps below:

- **Swipe upwards** from the **home screen.**
- Tap **Finder Search** at the top of your **apps page.**
- Next, enter the item you want to find in the search bar using keywords that accurately represents what you seek.

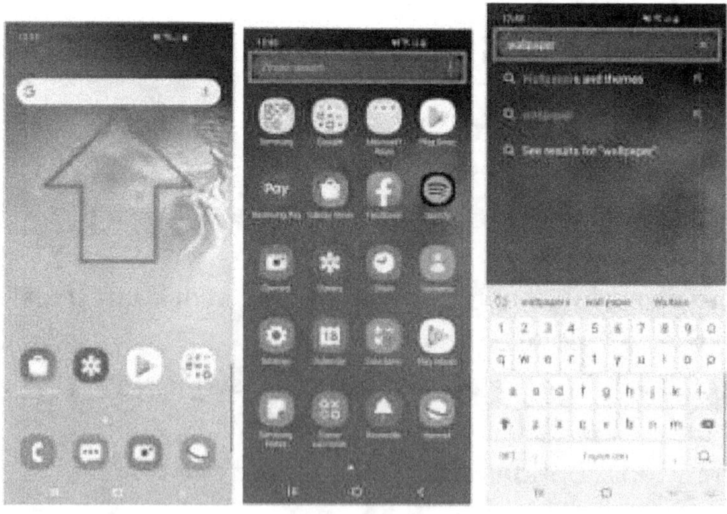

- Tap the **magnifying glass** in the keypad at bottom right edge of the screen.
- You will view contents relating to your search term from all compatible apps.
- If you can see what you seek, tap on it. If you can't, tap on **Search in app** to view more results.

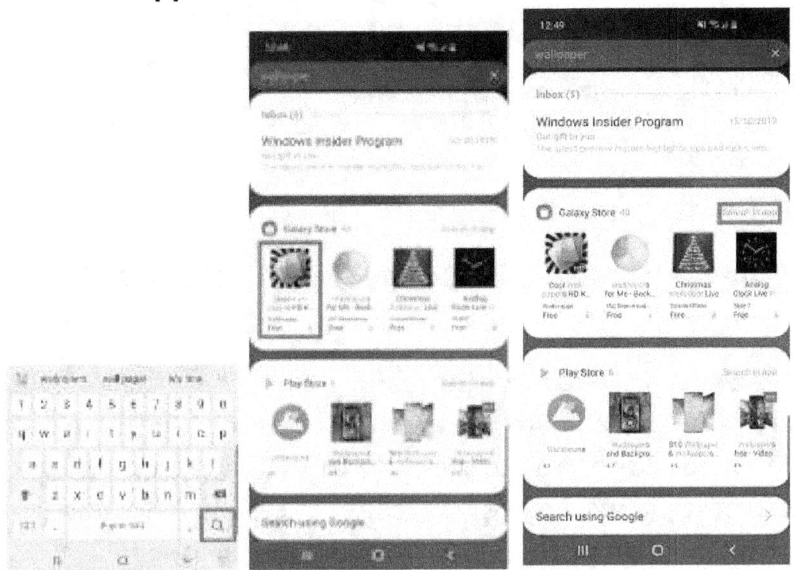

Quick Settings

This menu of your device allows you to easily and conveniently activate, deactivate or adjust specific settings or functions without going through a long procedure. Your S21 has a quick settings function that enables you to do just that by simply following the steps below:

- To access the quick settings menu, from two points, **swipe downwards** from the top of your S21.
- You would now view the quick settings menu. Currently active functions would be highlighted in blue.
- To view other functions and settings, **swipe left.**
- To return to the previous screen, **swipe right.**
- To activate or deactivate a quick setting function, **tap on it.**

Home Screen Customization

If you are not satisfied with the default outlay of your home screen, its possible for you to rearrange the apps to suit your preference, create folders to group apps, create new pages in case you download more apps and do much more. Just follow the guide below:

- To move an app, **tap and hold** the app icon.
- This action would launch an **information window** above the app. You are to still maintain your hold on the app.
- Move the app to a new position or location. You can opt to follow the **on-screen guide lines.**
- If you want move the app to a **new home screen,** move it to **edge of screen.**
- When you have the app in the new preferred location, **let go of the app** and it would stay there.

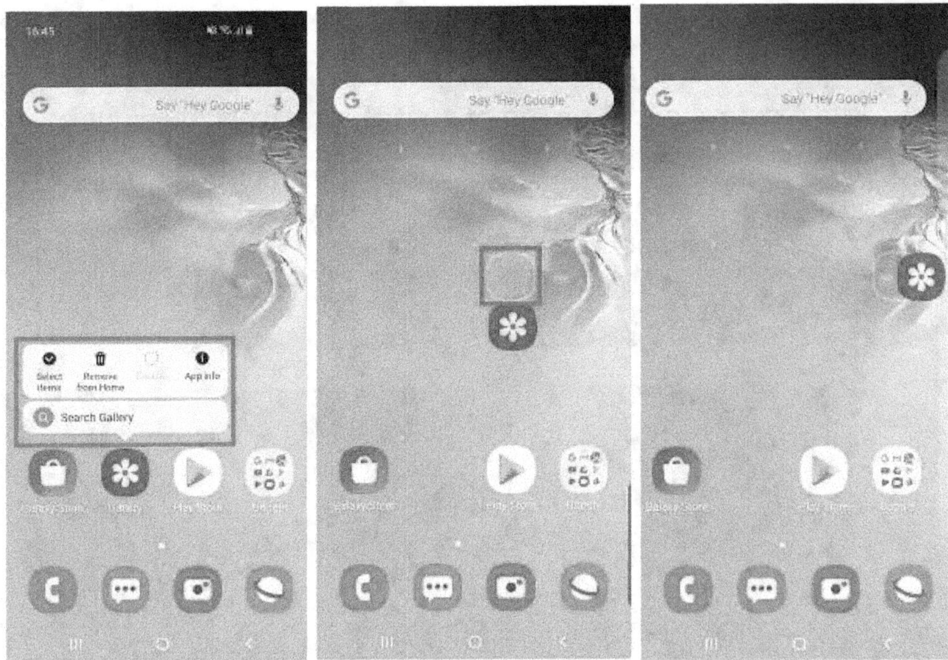

Addding an app icon to the home screen

- **Tap and hold the icon** till the information window comes into view.
- Next, tap **Add to Home.**

Creating a new folder

- **Tap and hold** an app icon.
- Next, **drag the icon on top of another app icon** you would want in the same folder.
- A grey outline should appear around the second app icon. Let go of the first app icon at this point.

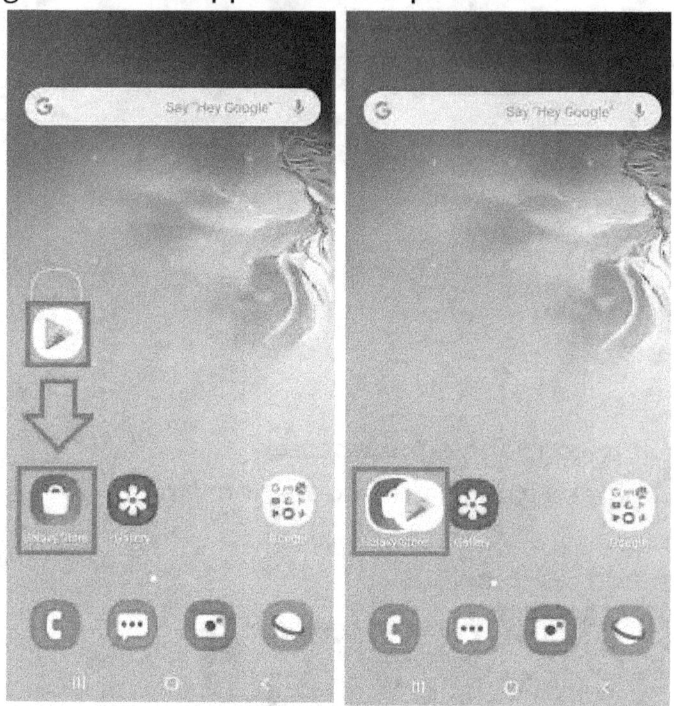

- Next, tap **Enter folder name** to give the new folder a new designation.
- If you want to populate the new folder with more appps, tap **Add apps** at screen bottom.

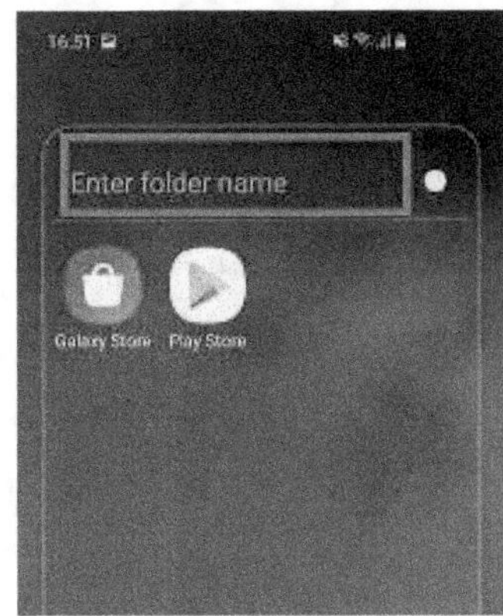

Creating more home screen pages

- From your home screen, **tap and hold a blank area.**
- Next, **swipe left** till you view a page with a plus (+) symbol at center.
- **Tap the plus symbol** to create a new home screen page.

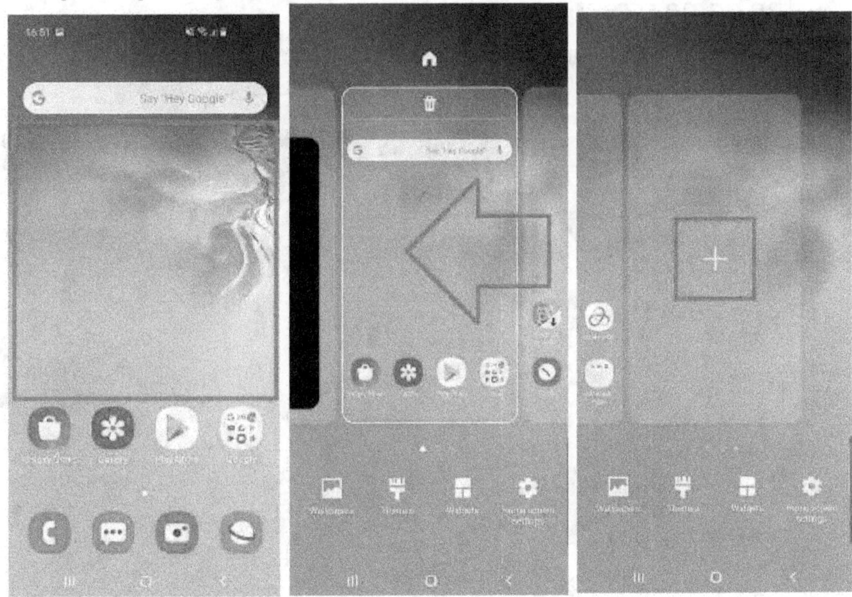

Adding Widgets to Home screen

- From your home screen, **tap and hold** a blank area.
- Next, tap **Widgets.**
- **Select the widget** you want to add.

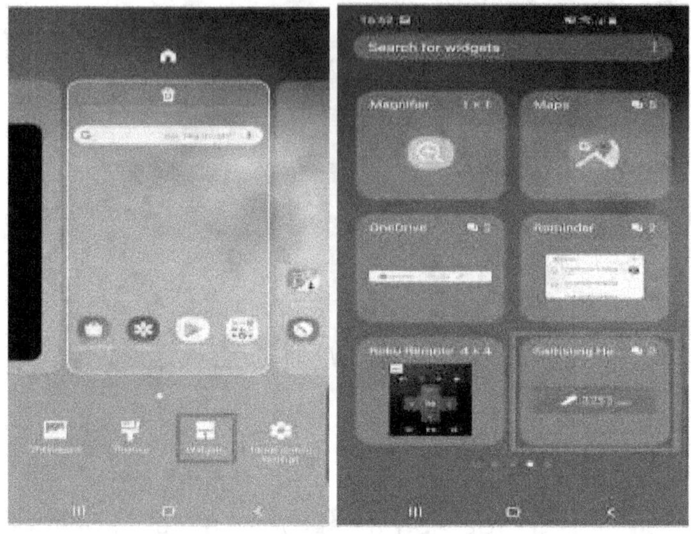

- If necessary, specify the size or type of widget you prefer.
- Next, **tap and hold the widget** you want in order to send it to the home screen.
- Place it in your preferred position by moving it around.
- Let go of the widget when you are satisfied.

Chapter 4: Wallpaper

If you don't like the wallpaper your S21 has by default, you can change it to one that you prefer. You have the option of selecting from one of the pre-loaded wall papers that came with your device or you can select an image from the ones you downloaded or taken yourself. To do so, follow the steps below:

Setting a wallpaper from the Home screen

- From the home screen, **tap and hold** an empty space.
- Next, **tap wallpapers** at far left of the icons towards the screen bottom.
- Based on your preference, you can now tap **my wallpapers** or **Gallery.** If you prefer to view more wallpapers, you can select **Explore more Wallpapers** at screen bottom.

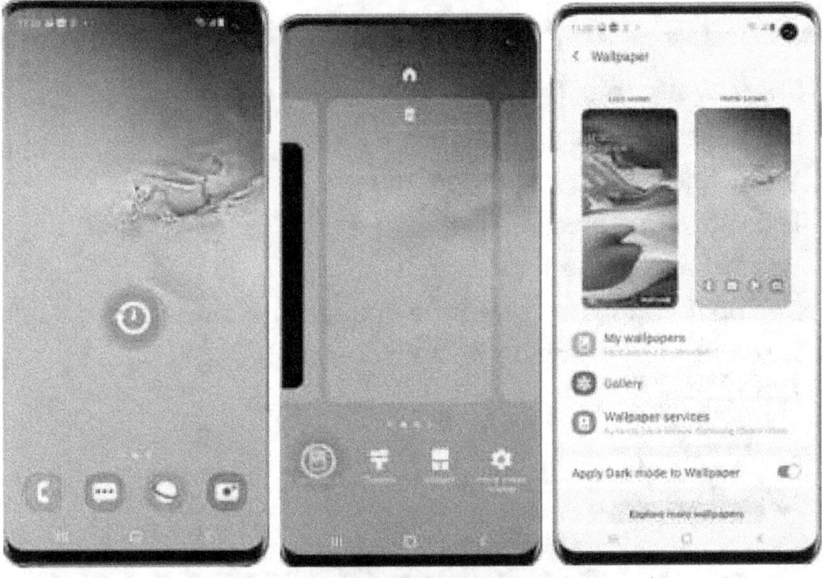

- Whether you chose **my wallpapers** or **Gallery**, tap the image you would want to use as your wallpaper and then tap **Done.**
- Next select whether to set the chosen image as the wallpaper for your **Home Screen, Lock Screen** or for both.
- Adjust the chosen image from the preview if you please and then tap **Set on Home Screen**, or **Set on Lock Screen** or **Set on Home and Lock Screen** to save your new wallpaper.

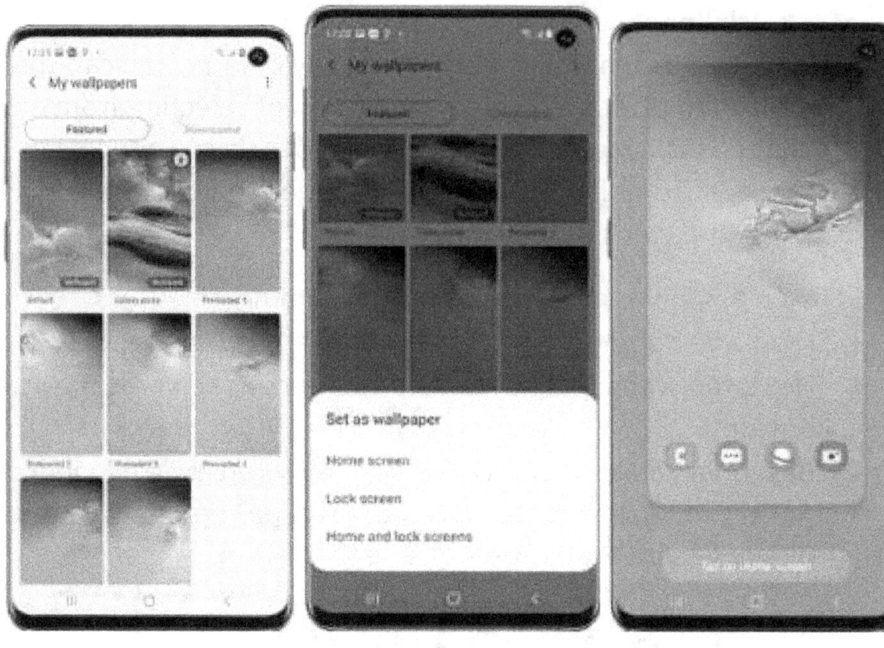

Setting a wallpaper from the device gallery

- Launch the **Gallery** app.
- Next, select **image or video** you prefer to use.
- Tap **more options.**
- Tap **Set as Wallpaper.**
- Decide if you want to use the image for **Home Screen, Lock Screen** or for **Home and Lock Screen.**

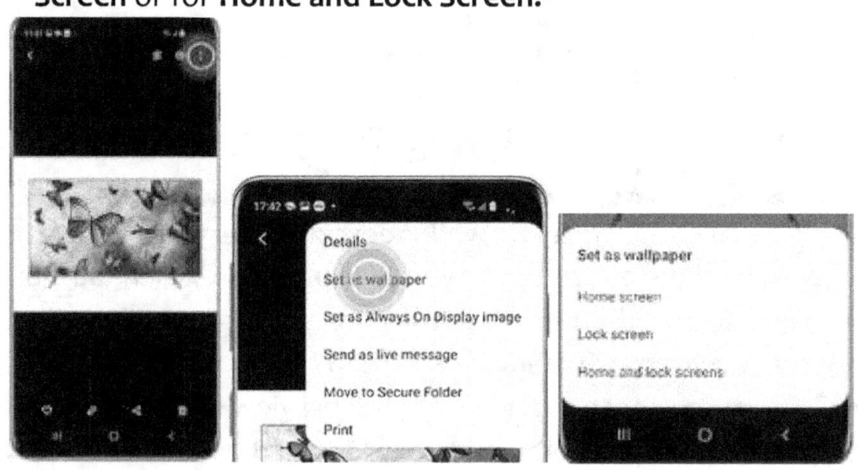

- From the next screen, which would be a preview of what the wallpaper would look like, you can adjust the position to suit your preference.
- When you are satisfied, choose from **"set on home screen"** or **"Set on Lock screen"** or **"Set on Home and Lock screens"** to save your preferred wallpaper.

Downloading a new wallpaper

If you don't find a wallpaper you like in the default or preloaded wallpapers on your S21, you can opt for downloading new ones. To do this, follow the steps below:

- First, from the home screen, **tap and hold** any empty space.
- Next, tap **wallpapers.**
- Then tap **Explore more wallpapers.**

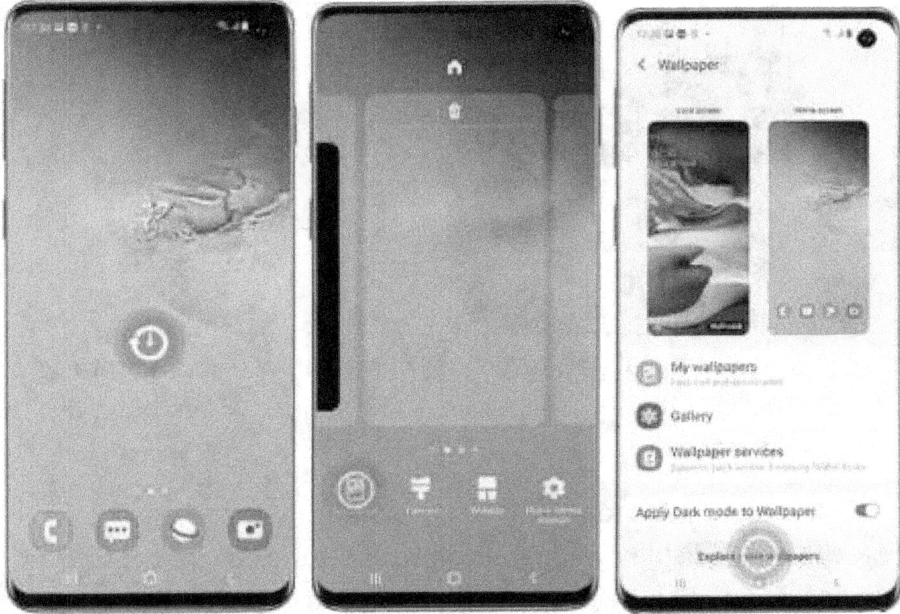

- From screen bottom, tap **wallpapers** and choose your preferred image.
- To view popular images, click **Top.**

- To search for a particular image, tap the **search icon** at **screen top right** and then search for a word. You also have the option of searching by colour palette or category.
- When you find a preferred image, you can tap on it to select and then tap **Download** at screen bottom.

- After the wallpaper has downloaded, you can now tap **Apply** to make it your wallpaper. To find more wallpapers, tap the back arrow.

Dynamic Lock Screen

The lock screen display wallpaper on your phone can be set to change periodically. To apply this setting, you have to activate the dynamic lock screen feature.

- Go to the wallpaper menu.
- Tap **Wallpaper services.**
- Next, tap **Dynamic Lock screen.**
- Tap **Apply.**

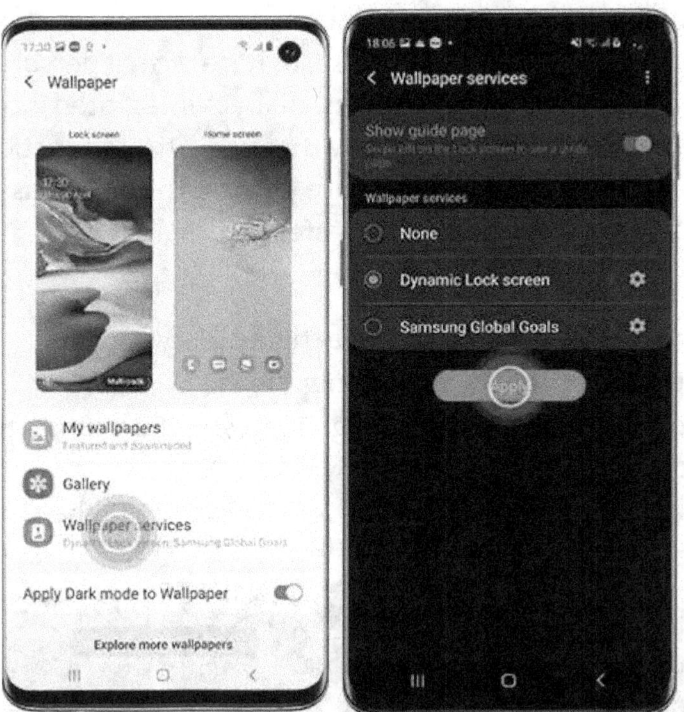

- Finally, tap the **Settings** icon and tap **Select category.**

Chapter 5: Bixby

Bixby is Samsung's answer to Apple's Siri. It's a virtual personal assistant that simplifies using your S21. Bixby is integrated into a lot of functions in your phone in such a way that using those functions are made flexible and accessible. The more you use the virtual assistant, the more it adjusts and learns your preferences.

Setting up Bixby

- First, press the **side key** to activate Bixby.
- At screen bottom, tap the **next** icon.
- You will be prompted to sign in to your Samsung account if you haven't done so already.
- Next, agree to terms and conditions and tap the **checkbox**.
- Tap the **next** icon again.

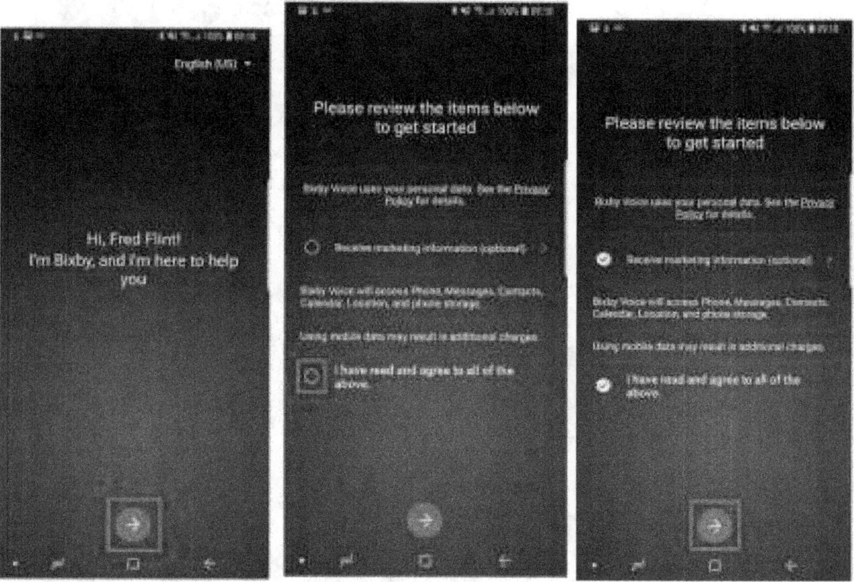

- At this point, you would view a tutorial of Bixby's functions and how to access them.

Using the side key to activate Bixby

- From the **Home screen,** swipe upwards to launch your apps.
- Launch the **Settings** app.
- Next, tap **Advanced Features**

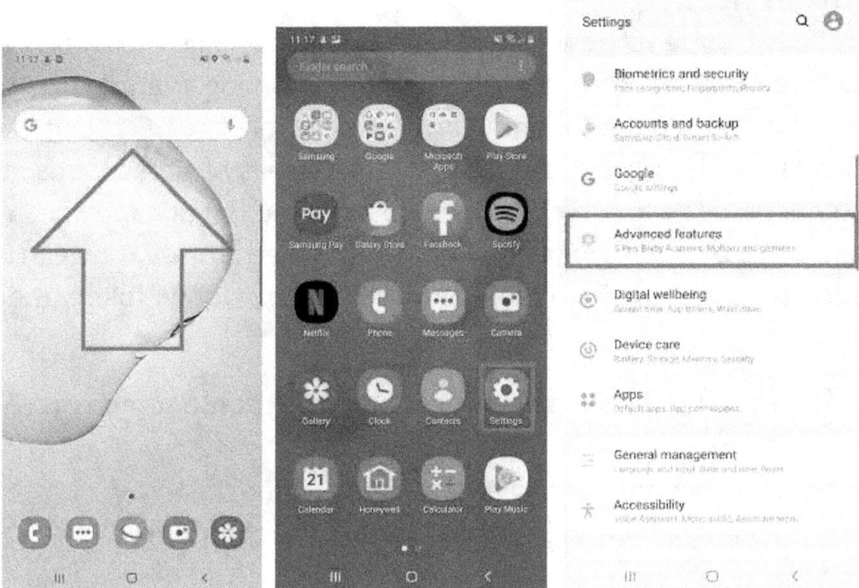

- Tap **Side key.**
- Tap **Open Bixby** if you want to use Bixby with a double press of the **side key**
- If you want to use Bixby by holding the **side key,** select **Wake Bixby**

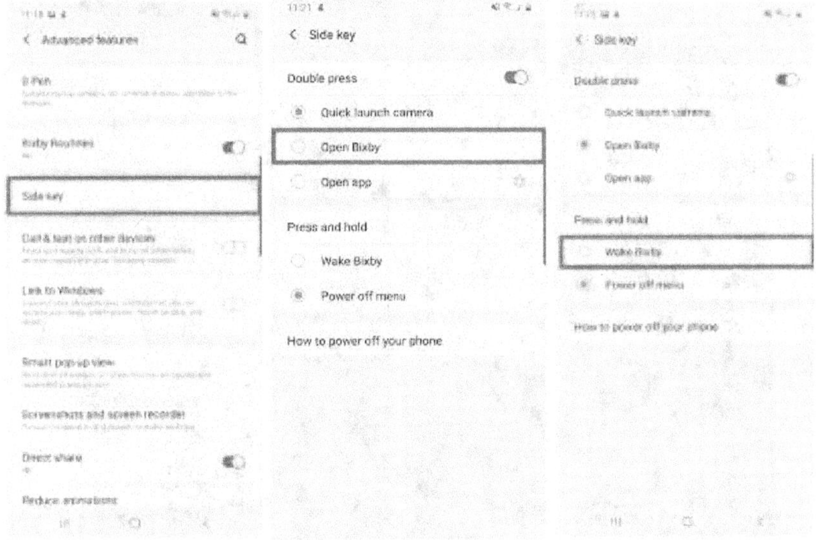

Bixby Home

Use Bixby Home to view information about stuff like the weather, news articles, get reminders about your upcoming events etc. Bixby Home is a homepage that regularly updates itself to reflect latest information. This information is displayed in easy-to-read cards. It's also possible for you to customize Bixby home to your specific preference by adding or removing what you get to see. You can equally decide to turn it off. To enable or disable Bixby Home, follow the steps below:

- **Touch and hold** a blank section of the **home screen** on your device.
- Next, **swipe right** to access Bixby Home.
- To enable or disable **Bixby Home**, tap the **switch.**

Using Bixby voice

- Press and hold the **side key**
- You would now view the **Bixby** logo on your screen display

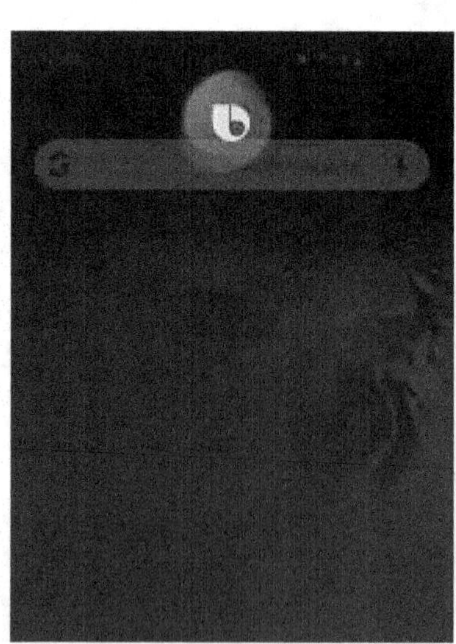
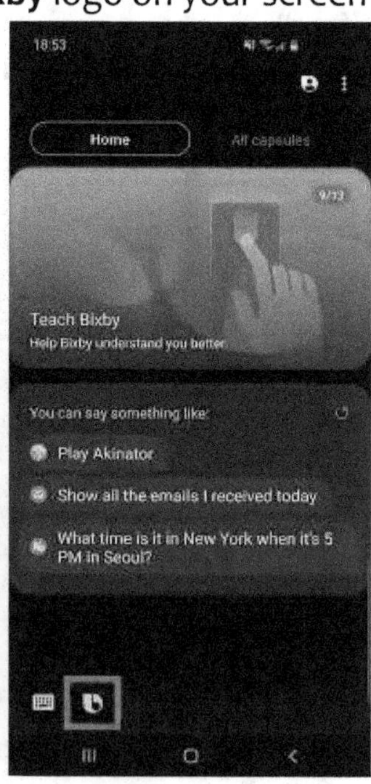

- Ask what you wish of Bixby

- When you are done and you wish to ask Bixby another question, tap the **Bixby icon** at screen bottom

Changing the Bixby voice language

- Use the side key to activate **Bixby**
- Tap the **menu** symbol. They are 3 dots at right side of screen
- Tap **Settings**

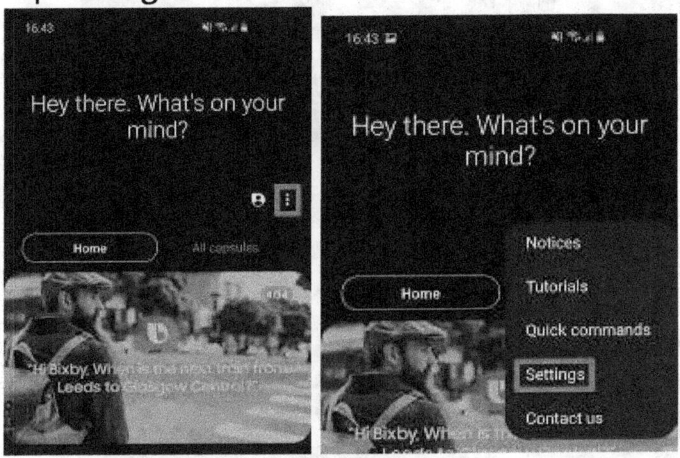

- Select **Language and voice style**
- Select **language**
- Finally, select your preferred language

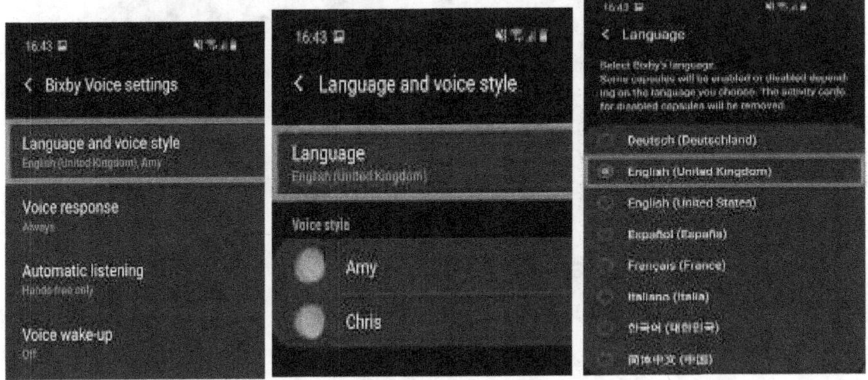

Using wake words to activate Bixby

If you would rather speak to wake Bixby than using buttons, especially if you are driving or using wireless headphones, you can activate this feature in your Bixby settings by doing the following:

- Use the **side key** to launch Bixby
- Tap the 3 dots **menu symbol** at screen upper right
- Select **Settings**

- Tap **Voice wake-up**
- Finally, tap the **switch** to activate voice wake up

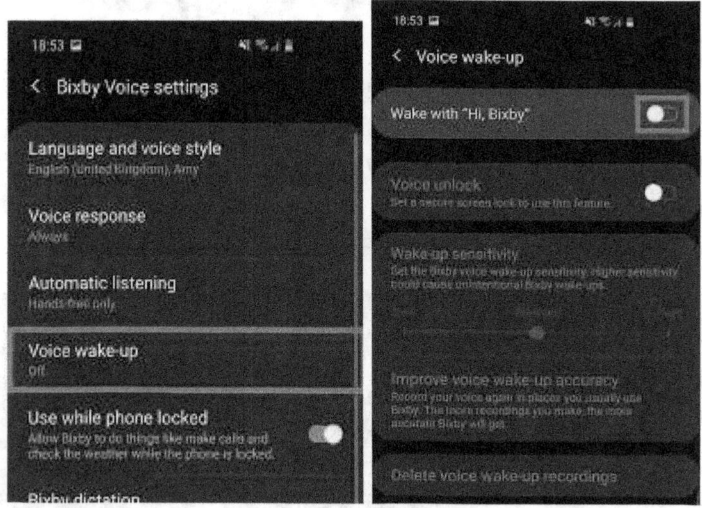

Using quick commands with Bixby

You can create a personalized command for Bixby. With this, you can actually compel Bixby to execute multiple commands just by a single word or phrase. To do this, follow the steps below:

- Use the **side key** to launch Bixby
- Next, tap the 3 dots **menu symbol** at screen upper right
- select **quick commands**

- tap a **command** to enable it or tap the **+** symbol to create a personalized one

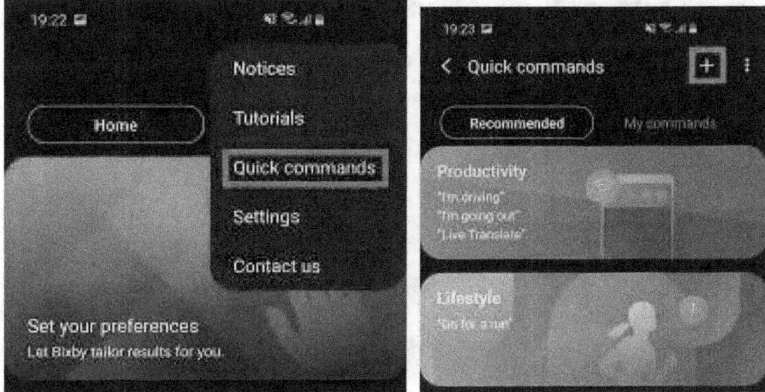

- enter the **activation word or phrase** you want to use
- tap **+ Add a command**

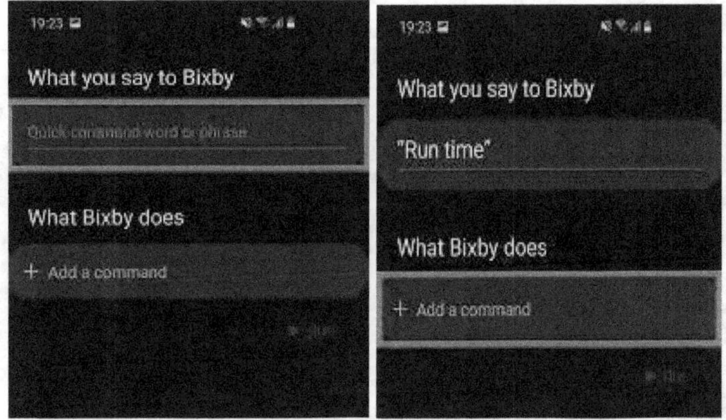

- enter a command by picking either by choosing from common commands, speaking a command or typing a command
- select the specific app you want to command

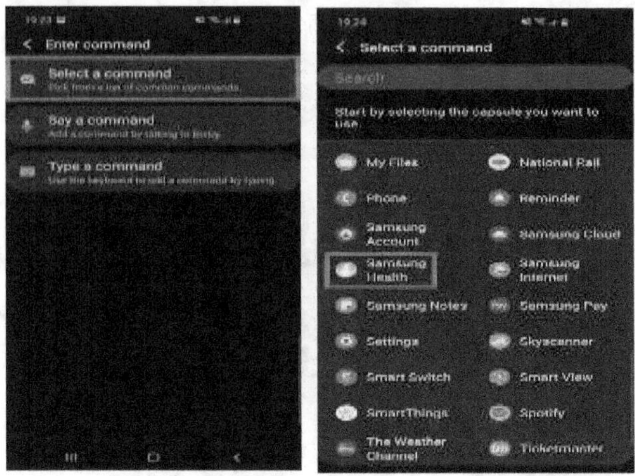

- choose the **command** you would prefer to use
- tap **+Add a command** to add another command to your quick command
- when you are satisfied with your quick command, tap **Save**

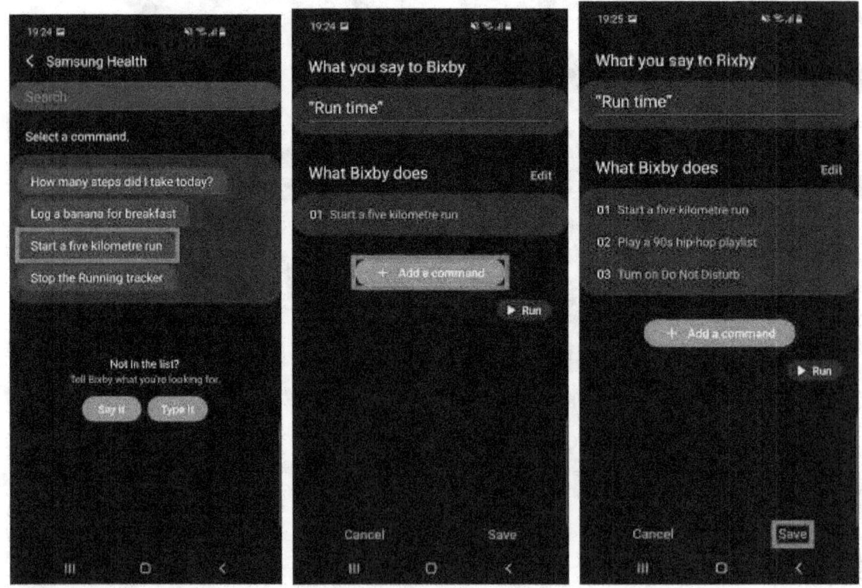

Adding cards to Bixby Home.

- Launch **Bixby** by **swiping right** from your **home screen.**
- Next, **tap the 3 dots** at **top right corner** to open the menu.
- Select **Cards.**
- Select the **app** whose card you want to display.

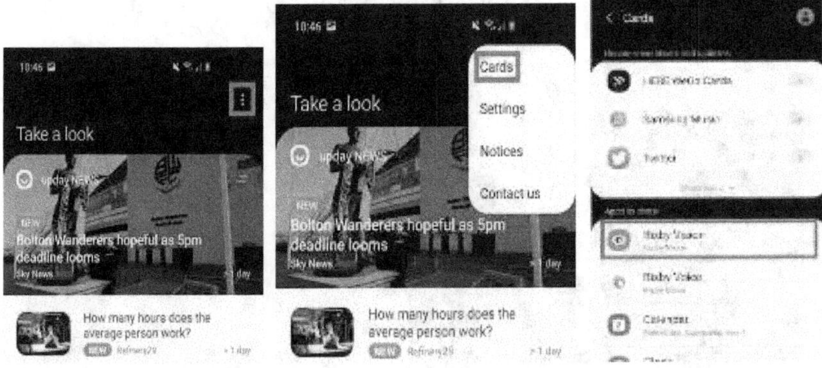

- Finally, tap the **switch** to activate or deactivate the apps card.

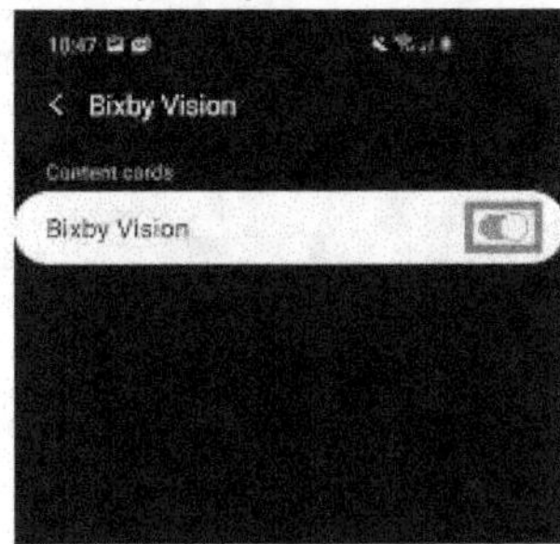

Managing cards on Bixby Home

You can control or specify how you get to view cards on Bixby Home. You do this by following the steps outlined below:

- Launch **Bixby Home** by **swiping right** from your home screen.
- Next, on the card you want to make changes to, tap the **menu** icon.
- If you want it to be at the top of your cards, tap **Pin to Top.**

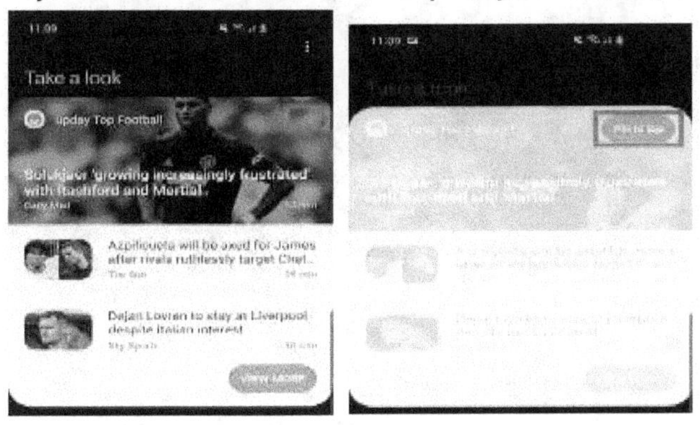

- If you want to hide a card, swipe right on it and tap **Hide for now.**

- If you prefer not to see it again, tap **Don't show again**

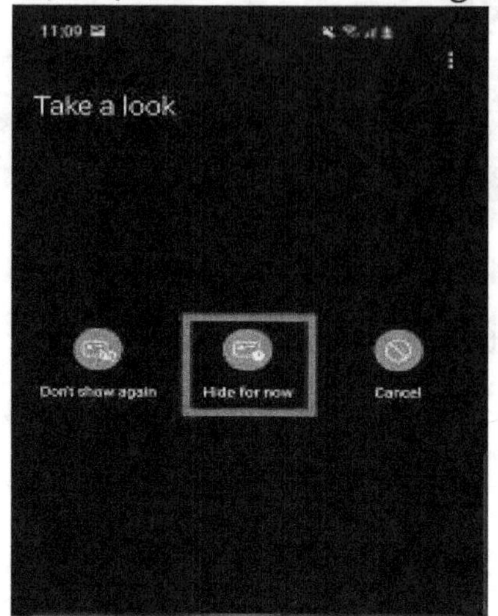

Activating or deactivating Bixby Routines

If you use Bixby regularly, it learns and adapts to your specific usage patterns and choices. It can now automatically adjust your settings at set times and do much more. To turn on or turn off Bixby routines, follow the steps below:

- From the Home screen, **swipe upwards** to view your apps.
- Next, tap **Settings.**
- Select **Advanced features**.
- Finally, tap the **switch** to turn Bixby routines on or off.

Using a Bixby recommended routine

Bixby would start suggesting some routines for you when it adapts to your usage procedure. This would come as notifications that show at top of your home screen display. In the eventuality that you decide to use a Bixby suggested routine, you would need to add it to your routines by following these steps:

- When the suggested routine appears as a notification at screen top, **swipe down** from screen top
- Next, tap on the **notification card** to view more

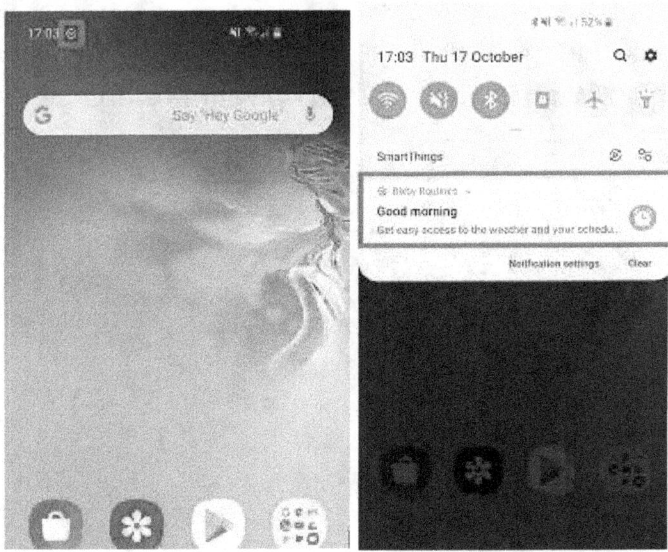

- Select **View all.**

- Tweak the routine to your choice and tap **Save routine.**

Using a preset Bixby routine

- Access your apps by **swiping upwards** from home screen
- Next, tap **Setting**
- Tap **Advanced features**
- Tap **Bixby routines**
- Tap **recommended**

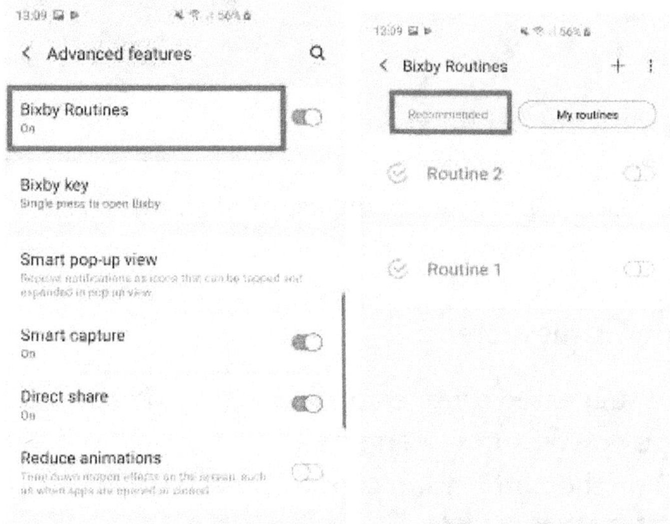

- Select a **routine** from the list
- Tweak the **"if "** and **"Then"** based on your preference

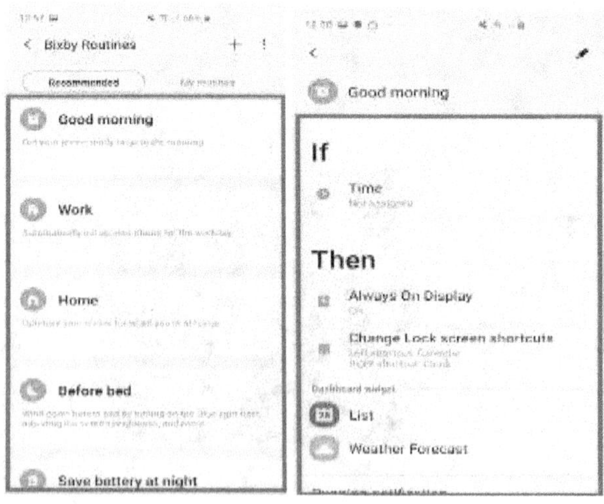

- Tap **Save routine**
- You should be able to view the new routine in **My routines**

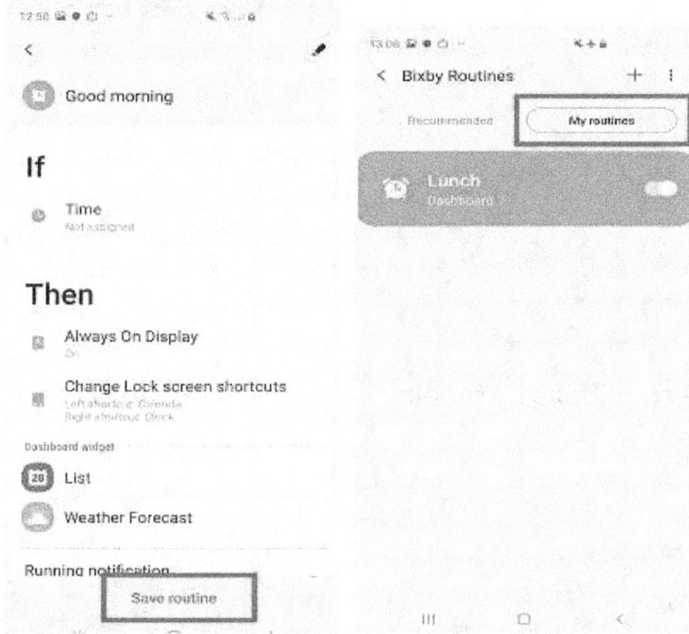

Customizing a Bixby routine

- Access your **apps** from the home screen
- Tap **Settings**
- Tap **Advanced Features**
- Tap **Bixby routines**
- Tap the + icon
- Type a **name** for your routine

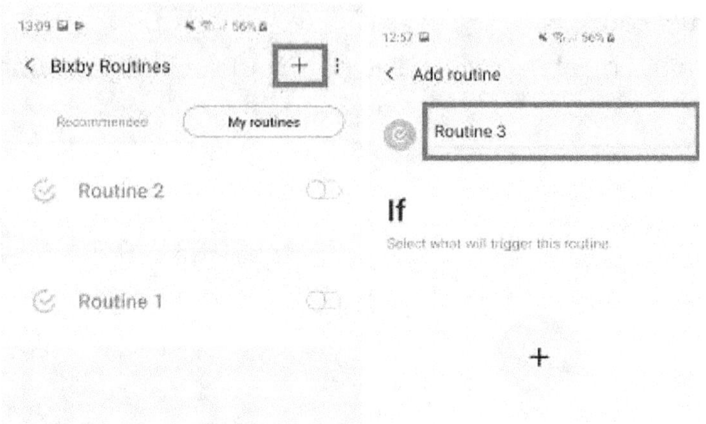

- Set the conditions by tapping + again and tap **next** at screen bottom

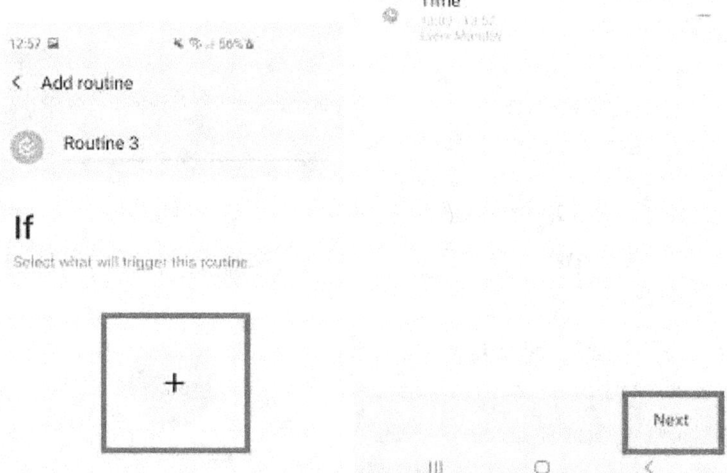

- Tap the + icon again to specify the action
- Tap **Done** at bottom of screen
- You should see the new routine in **My routines**

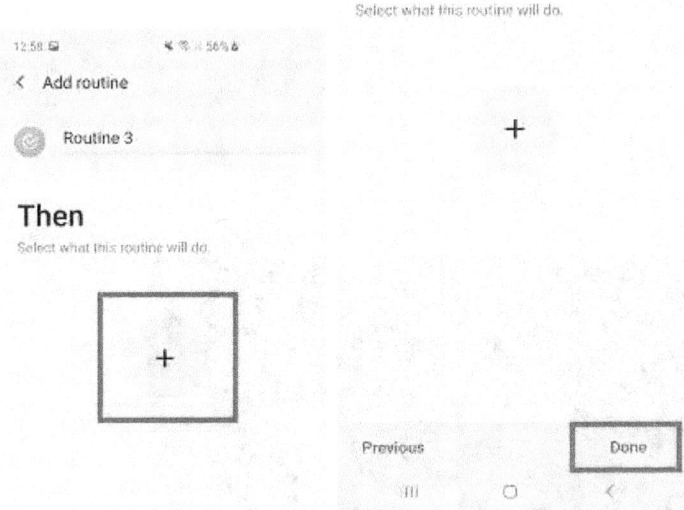

Deactivating a routine

- Launch **apps** from home screen
- Tap **Settings**
- Tap **Advanced features**
- Tap **Bixby Routines**
- Tap **My routines**

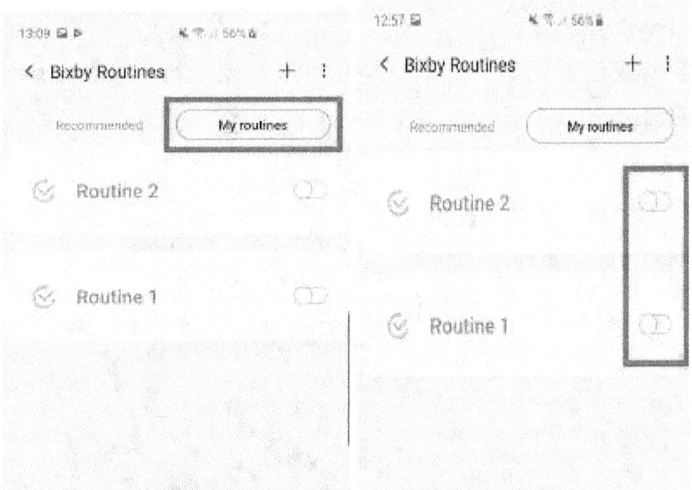

- To deactivate a live routine, **swipe down** from screen top to view the **notifications panel**
- Select the **Bixby Routines** notification and tap **Stop**

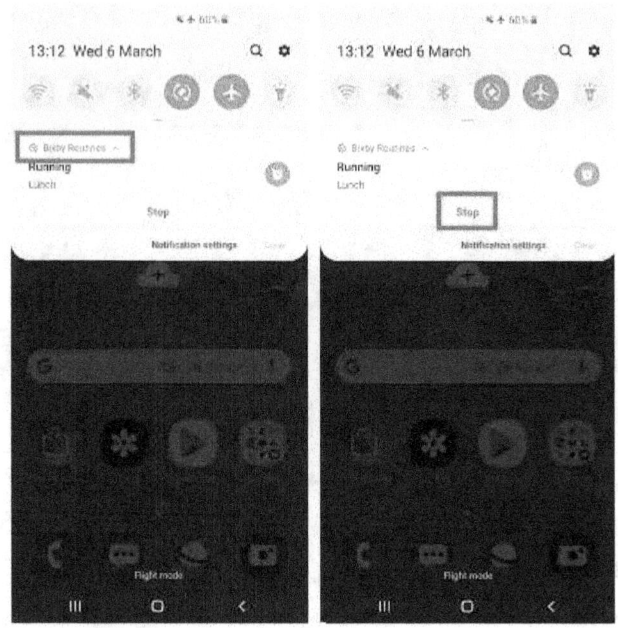

Removing a Bixby Routine

- Launch **apps** from home screen
- Tap **Settings**
- Tap **Advanced features**
- **Tap Bixby Routines**
- Tap the **menu** icon that shows as 3 dots at screen upper right
- Select **Delete**

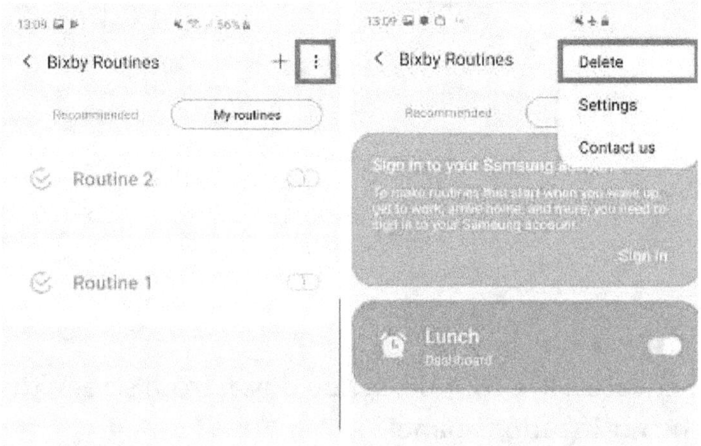

- Specify the particular **routine** you want to delete or tap **select all** as the case applies
- Finally, tap **Delete at** screen bottom to execute the action

Changing the default digital assistant

The S21 by default comes with google assistant but you can change it to another of your choice or preference such as Bixby, Finder, Samsung internet etc. you can even totally turn off the digital assistant feature if you wish.

- **Swipe down** from screen top to open the notifications shade
- Select **Settings**
- Navigate down and tap on **apps**
- Next, tap on **Choose Default Apps** at top of display

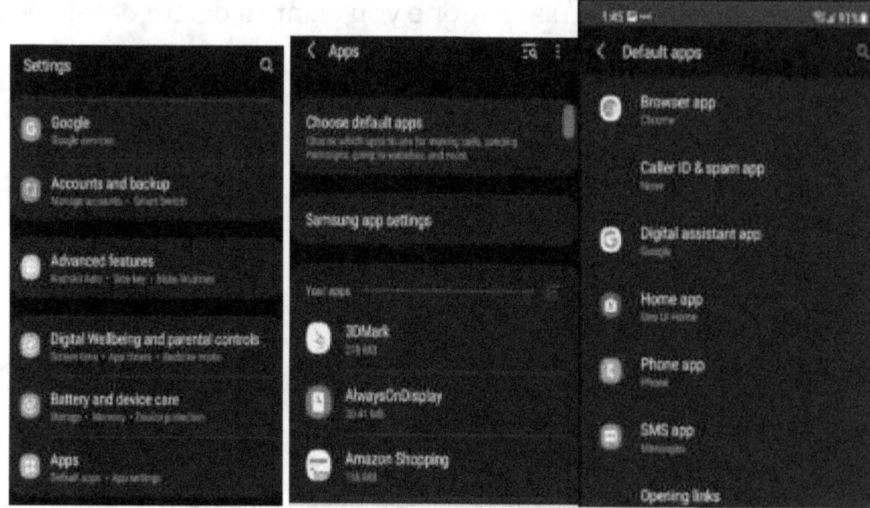

- Select **Digital Assistant app**
- **Tap on the phone assistant app**

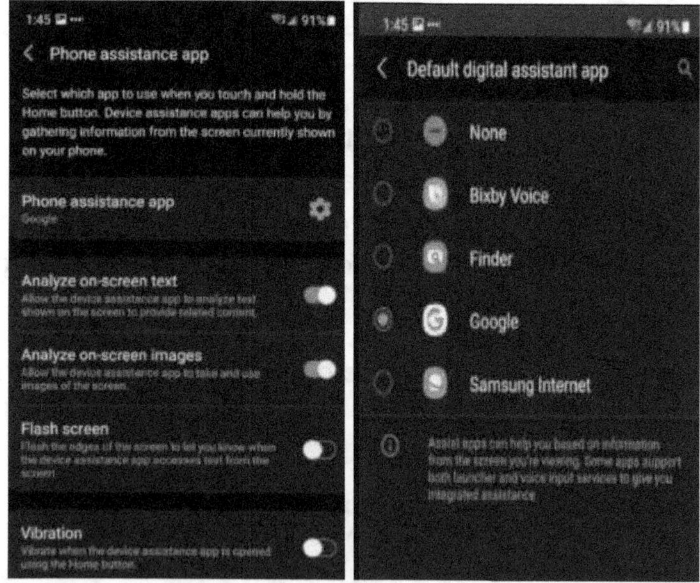

- Select an option from the list

Chapter 6: contacts

When it comes to contacts, there are several ways to get your contacts on your new S21. If you are switching to your s21 from a smartphone, you can back up your contacts on your google account along with other stuff and transfer them to your new device. You could also do this via the Samsung smart switch app. This has already been covered in the first chapter. If this is your first smart phone and you happened to be using a non-smart phone previously, an option would be to move your contacts on the non-smart phone to your sim before transferring the sim to the S21 and then moving the contacts to the S21 internal storage capacity; though its advisable to create a google account and back the contacts up there in case you need to switch phones again. You could also transfer your contacts via Bluetooth or you can also save contacts from scratch. For any of the options you decide to use, find the steps outlined in this chapter.

Creating a personal contacts profile for your S21

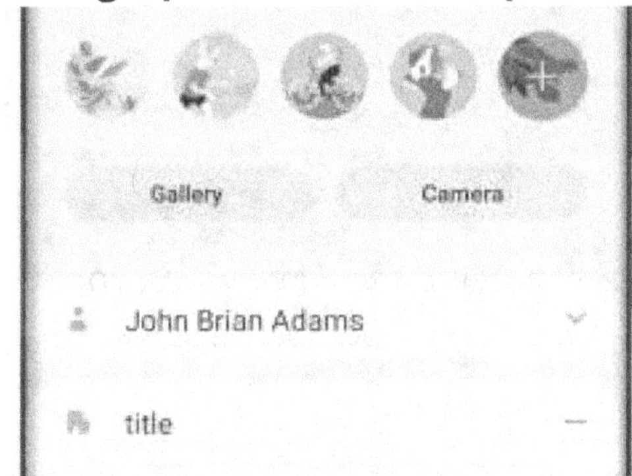

- Launch your **contacts** app
- Next, tap the **profile picture** at screen top
- You may have to sign in to your Samsung account
- If you wish to edit your information, tap **Edit** at screen bottom
- When you are done entering your information, tap **Save** at the bottom right-hand corner

Adding a new contact

- From the apps display, launch the **contacts** app
- Next, tap the + symbol at bottom of screen
- Select where you want to save the contact

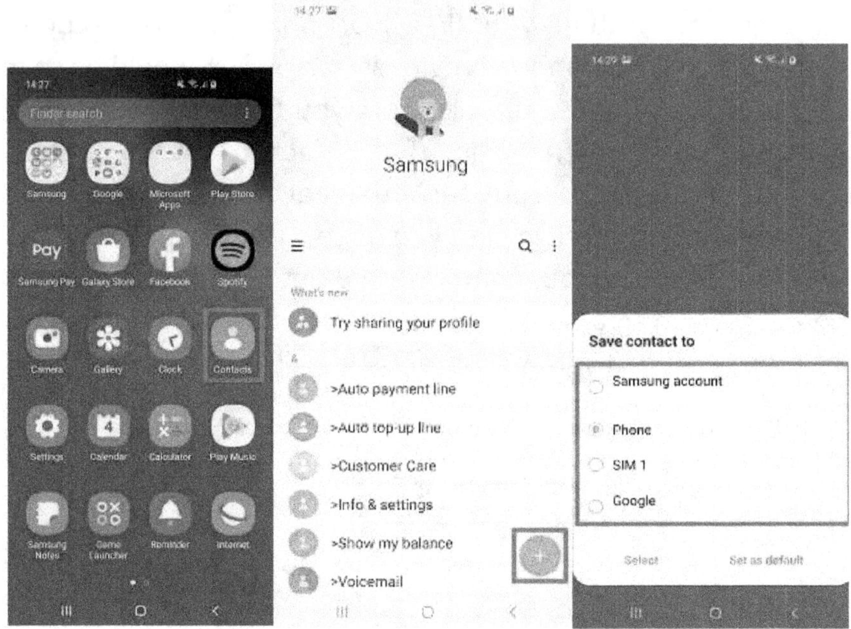

- Enter the details of the contact and tap **Save** when you finish

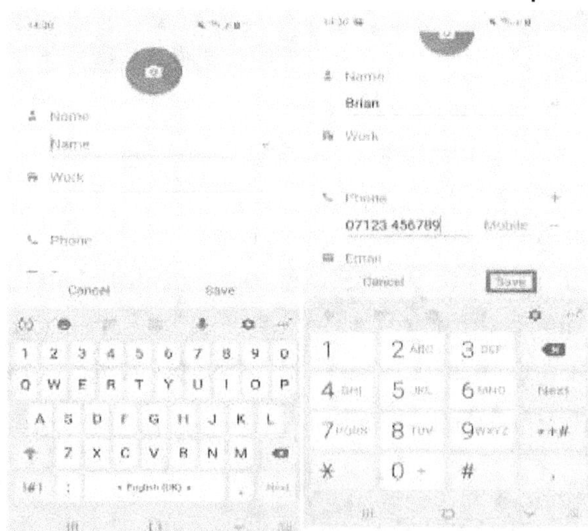

Editing a contact

- Choose the contact to be edited
- Tap on **Edit** at screen bottom
- Next, **tap view more** to view all information you can edit

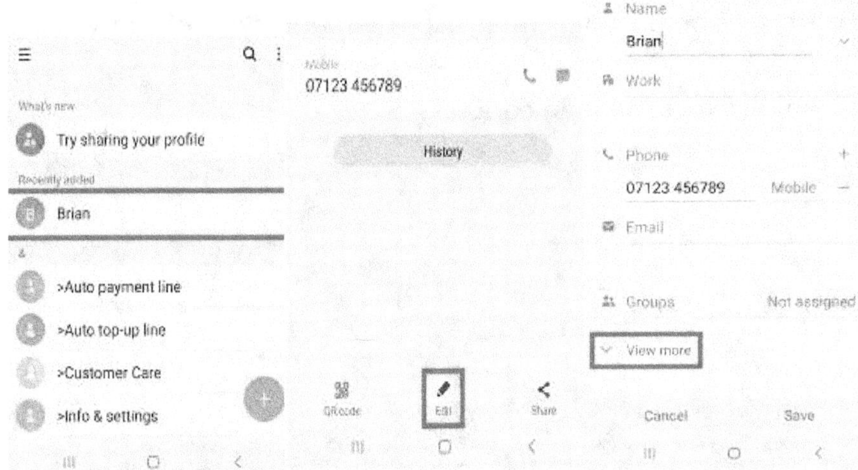

- Tap on **any section** to edit it
- Tap **Save** to finish when done

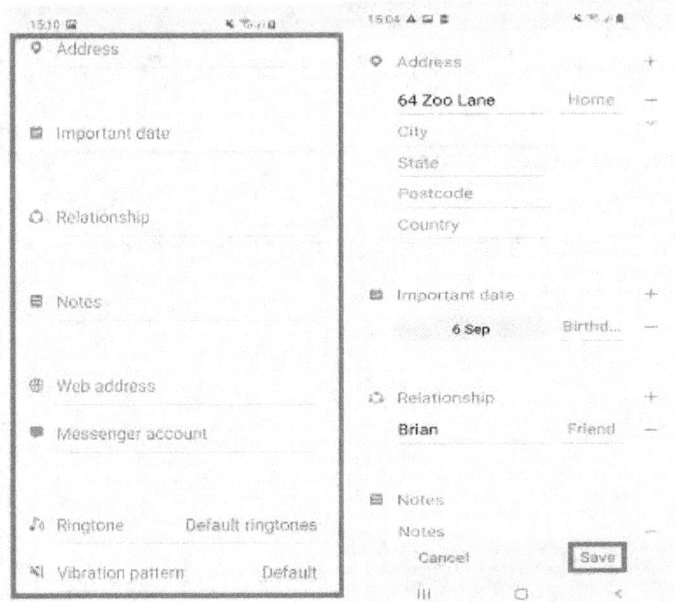

Moving your contacts to your S21 from your SIM card

Before you do this, you would have transferred your contacts to your SIM card from your previous device.

- Launch your **contacts** app
- From upper left of screen, tap the **menu symbol** shown as 3 lines
- Next, select **Manage contacts**

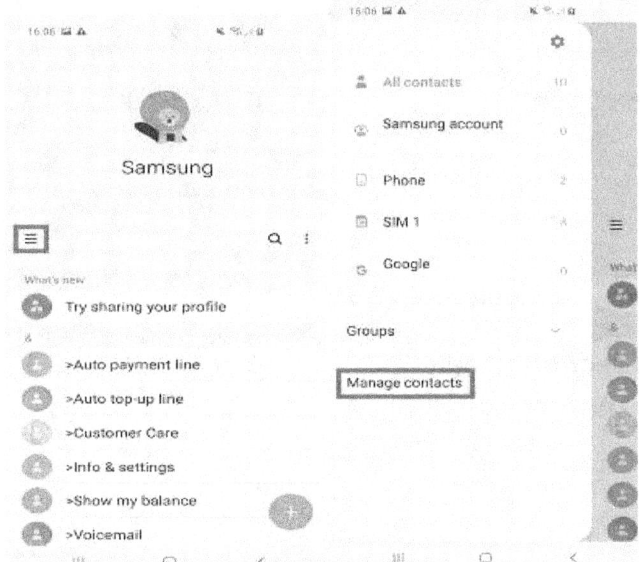

- Select **Import/export contacts**
- Since you are transferring from your SIM to phone, tap **Import**
- Choose from where the contacts are to be moved

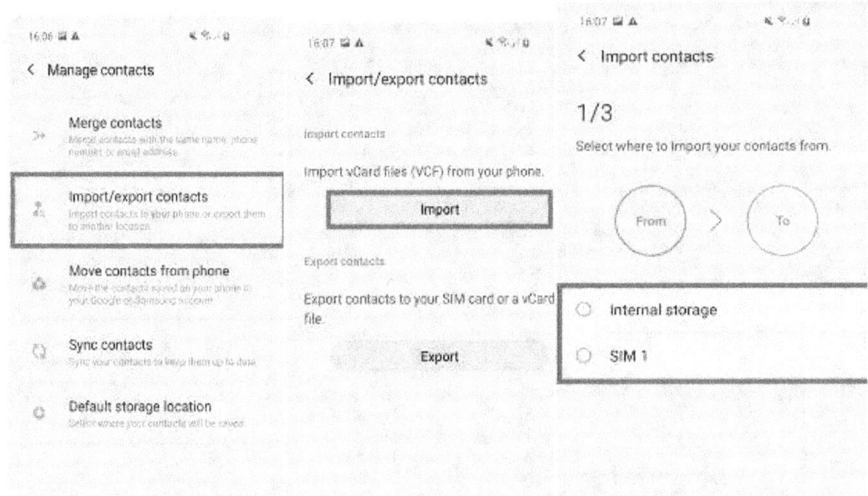

- Select the contacts to be imported and tap **Done**

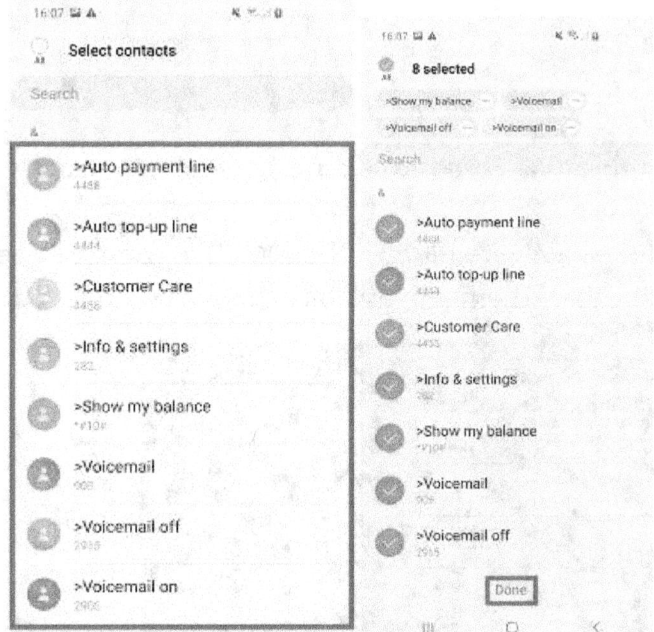

- Specify where the imported contacts are to be stored or saved
- Next, tap **Import** to move the contacts

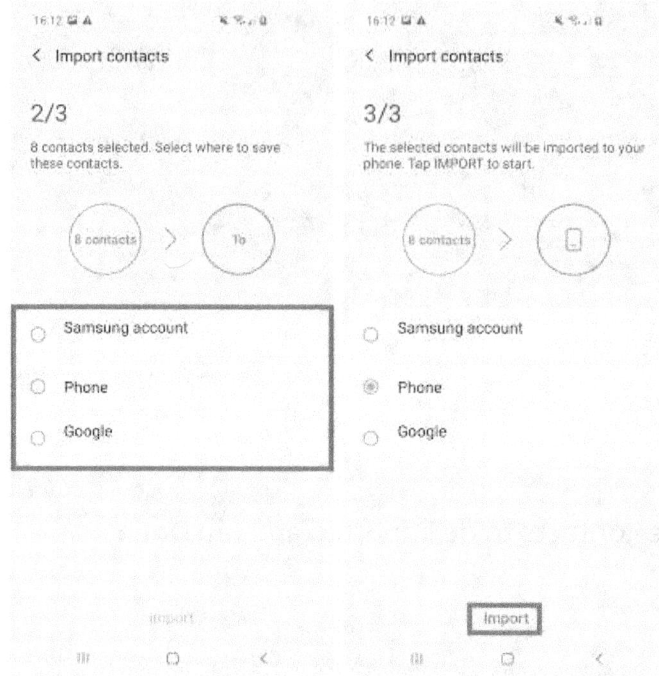

Using bluetooth or Wi-Fi to move data from old Samsung to your S21

- From **Settings,** activate Bluetooth or Wi-Fi for both devices
- Next, pair both of them and establish a secure connection

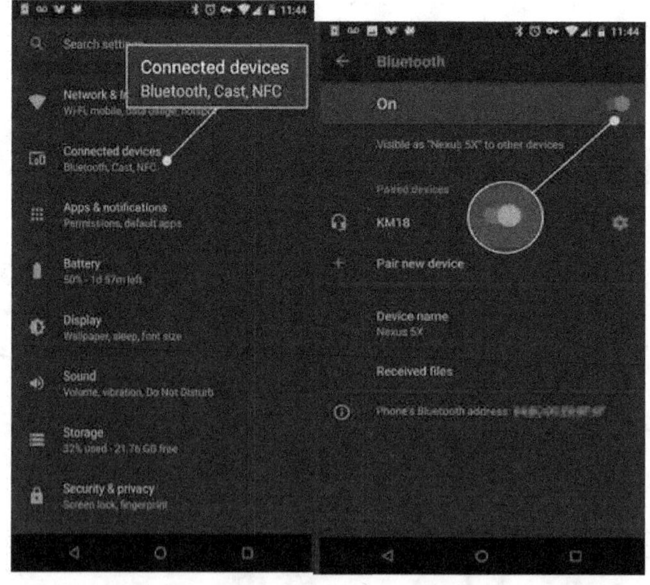

- When you have established a connection, from the old device or source phone, go to **Contacts** and select if you want to transfer all or specific contacts
- Next, go to **share options** and decide to send contacts via Bluetooth or Wi-Fi
- Finally, select the connected device and accept the incoming data or contacts

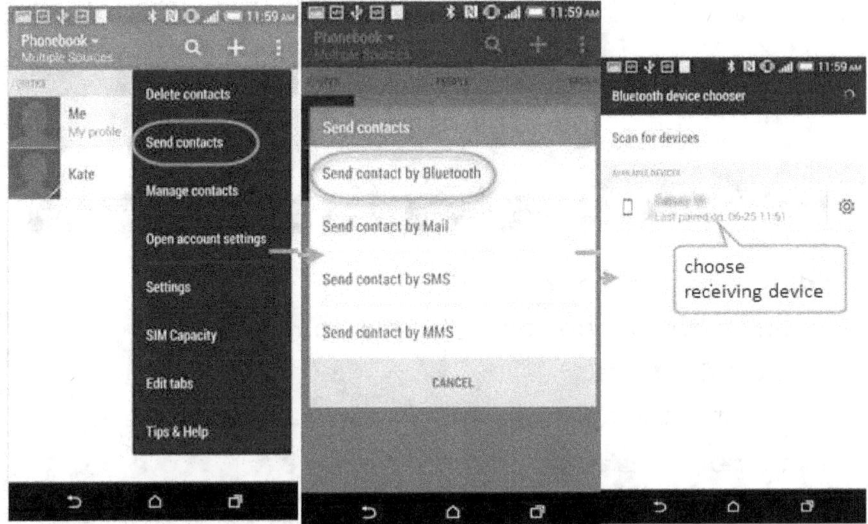

- When the transfer is done, you can unpair both devices by going to **Settings** next to the paired devices and tapping **Unpair**

Using Google back-up to transfer contacts from old device to S21
- Ensure that both devices are linked to the same google account
- Next, go to the **Google account settings** of your old device and activate the option to sync contacts
- Do the same for your S21
- Your contacts would sync automatically to your new device
- You can also download the **Google contacts** app on both devices
- Make sure that your **contacts** on your old device is imported to the **Google contacts app**
- The app would automatically sync your contacts and allow you to access them on both devices

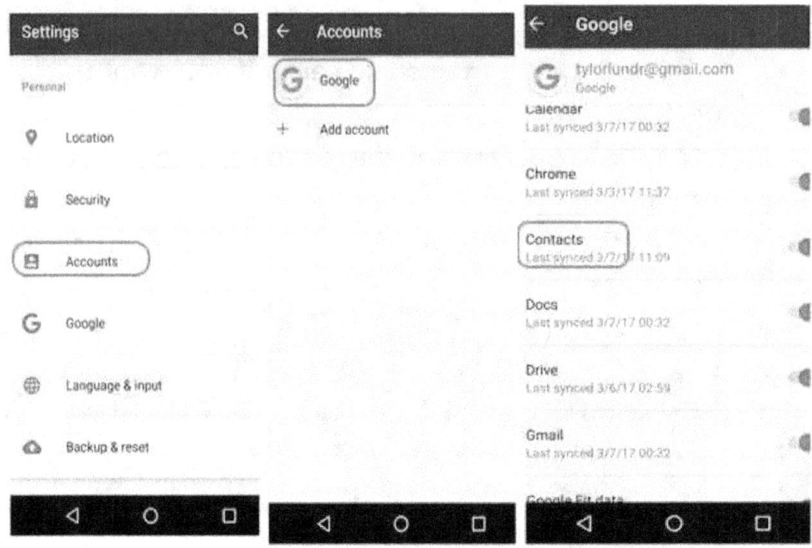

Adding a contact to speed dial

- Launch the **phone app** from your home screen
- Select **Contacts**
- Next, tap the **options** symbol shown as 3 dots

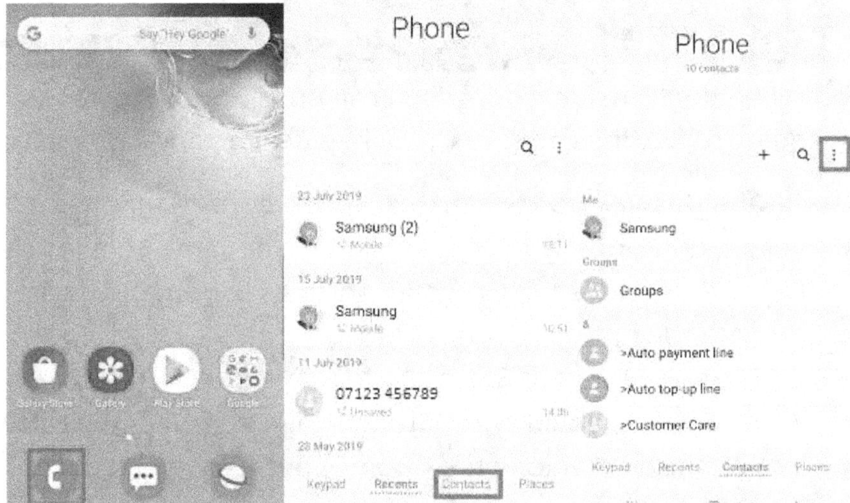

- Select **Speed dial numbers**
- Next, tap the **down arrow** to change the speed dial number
- Enter the **phone number** or tap the **contact symbol** to enter the contact information

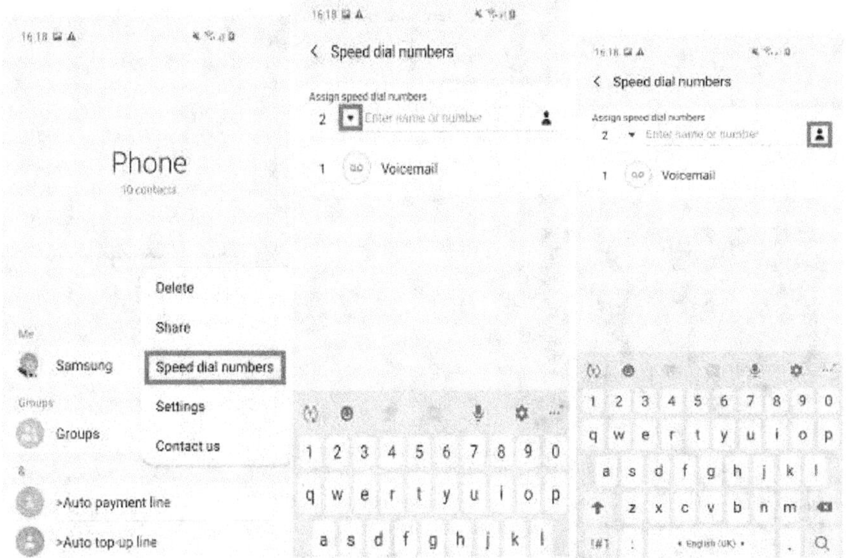

- If you wish to delete a speed dial number, tap the – next to the number

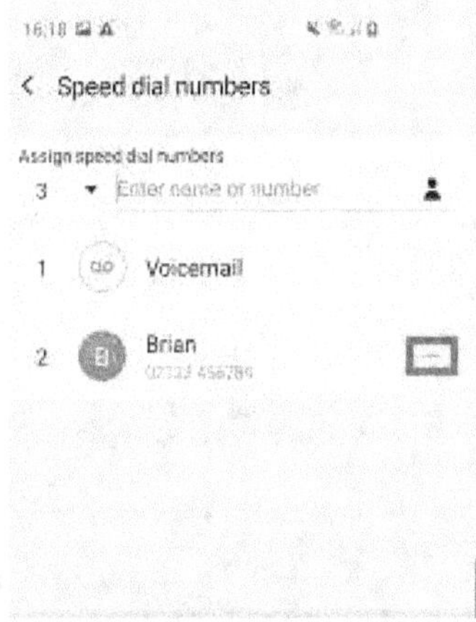

- To use a speed dial, **press and hold** the **number** assigned to the **contact** you want to call on the **keypad**

Calling a contact

- Launch the **apps page**
- Tap **Contacts**
- **Scroll up or down** to find and select the required contact
- Tap the **call symbol** next to the required SIM

- Tap the **end call** symbol to terminate the call when you are done

Creating a caller group

- Launch the **contacts** app
- Tap the **menu symbol** shown as 3 lines at upper left of screen
- Tap **Groups**
- Select **Create group**
- Enter a **name** for the group

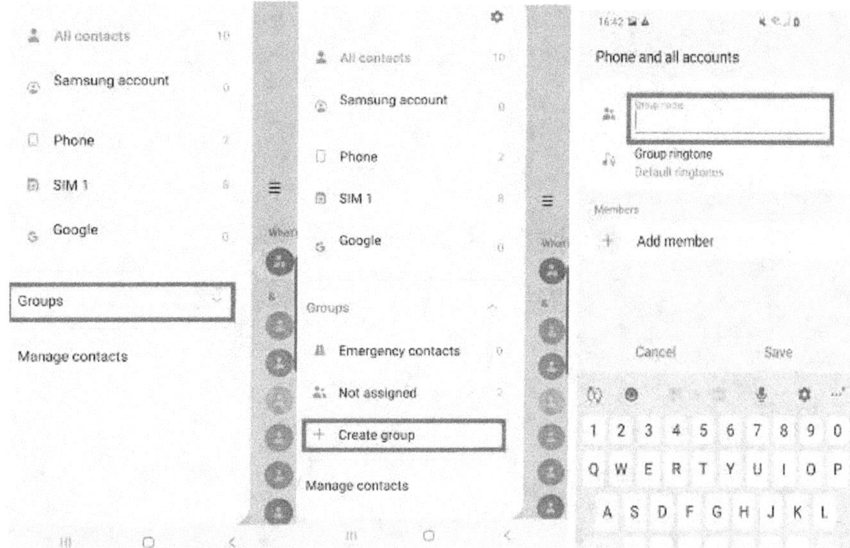

- Tap on **Add member**
- Choose the **contacts** to be added to the group

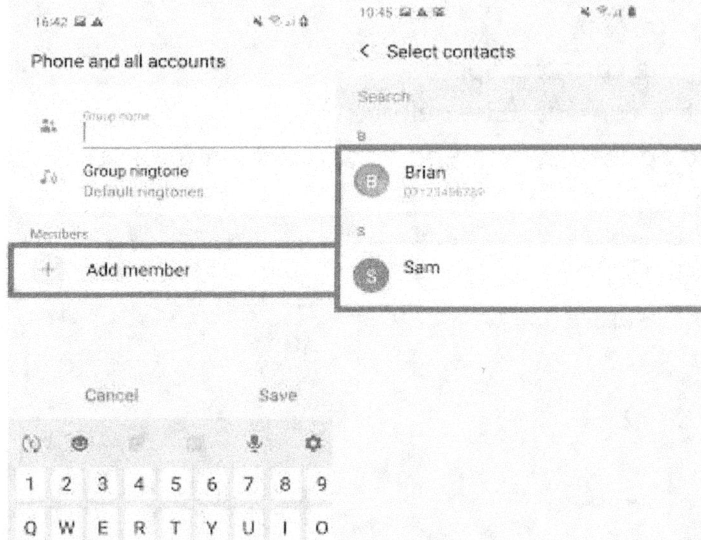

- Tap **Done**
- Finally, tap **Save**

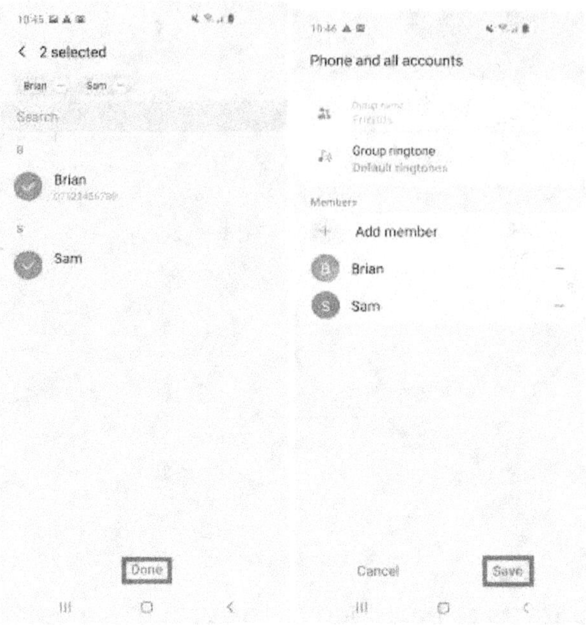

Deleting a contact

- Launch the **contacts** app
- Select the **contact** to be deleted
- Tap the **options** symbol shown as 3 dots at upper right of screen

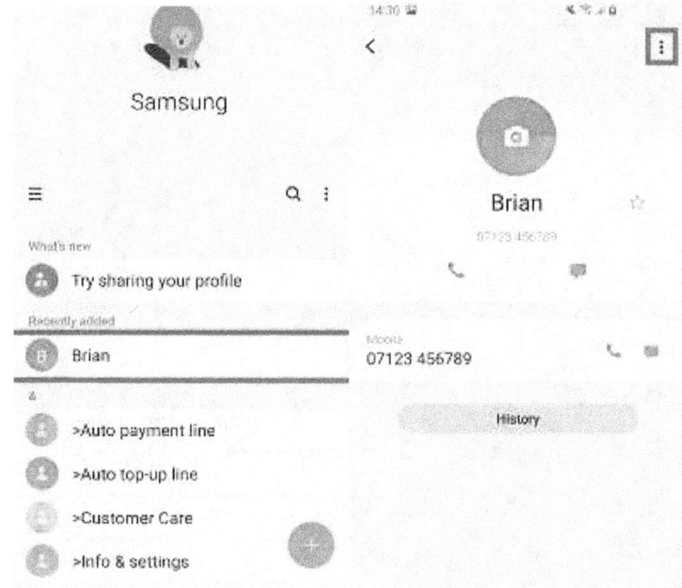

- Next, tap **Delete**
- Tap **Delete** again to confirm

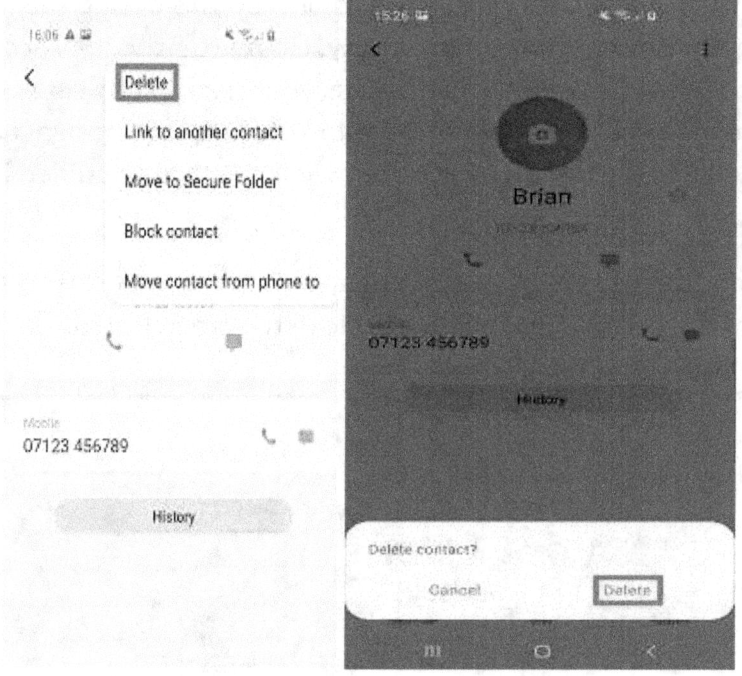

Chapter 7: Mail

Before you can start using effectively, the mail feature of your phone, you have to first of all, set it up. If you didn't do this during the initial set-up of your device, you can do it now. No matter the mail account or service provider you use, you can access your mail just by setting it up on your new device and your mail would automatically be synced to your S21. All this is possible by just following the steps outlined below:

Adding an email Account

- From top of screen, **swipe down** to launch quick settings
- Next, tap **Cloud and accounts** close to screen bottom
- Select **Accounts**

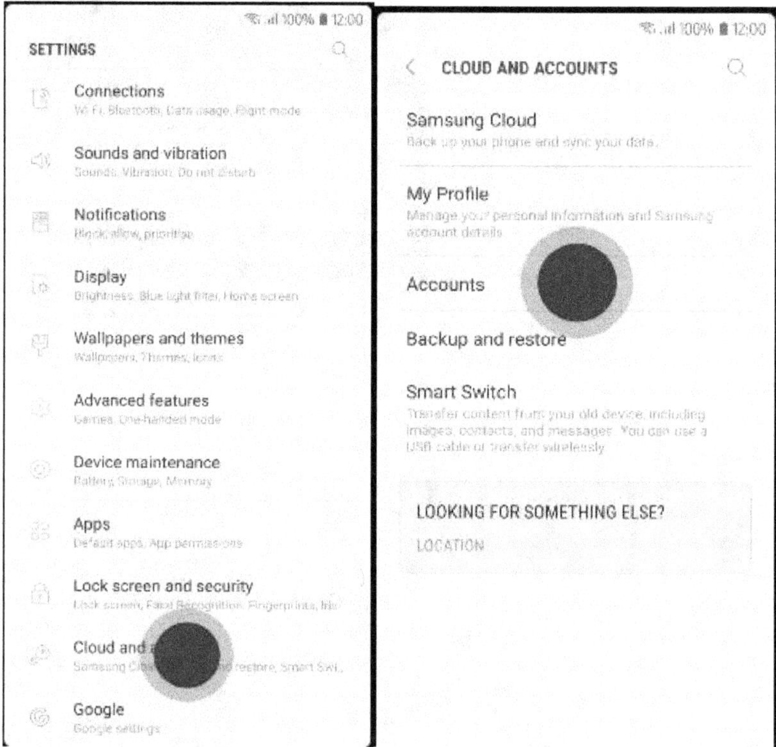

- Tap **Add account**
- Tap **Email**
- Enter your email **user name and password** to log in

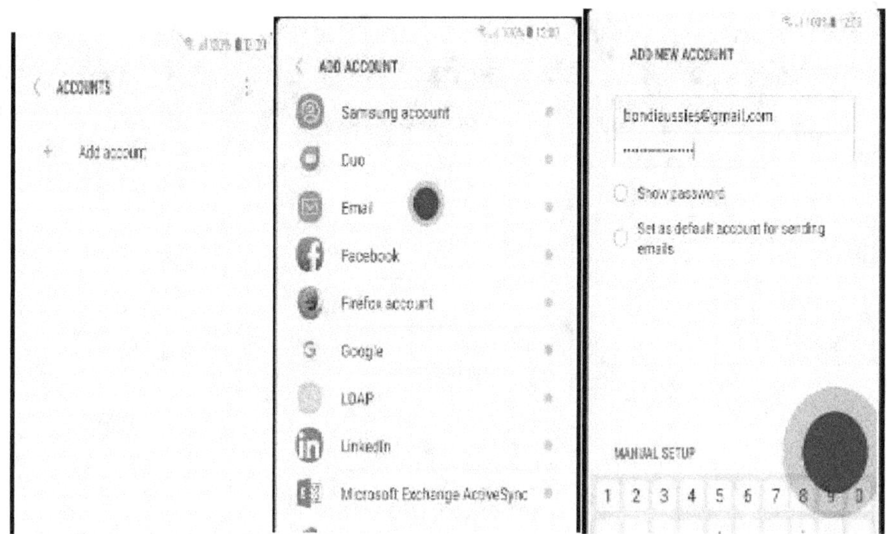

Setting up a google account

- Launch quick settings by **swiping down** from screen top
- Tap **Cloud and accounts**
- Tap **Accounts**
- Select **google**
- Tap on **Create new account** or enter your **email and password** if you already have a google account
- Key in your **first and last name** and then tap **Next**

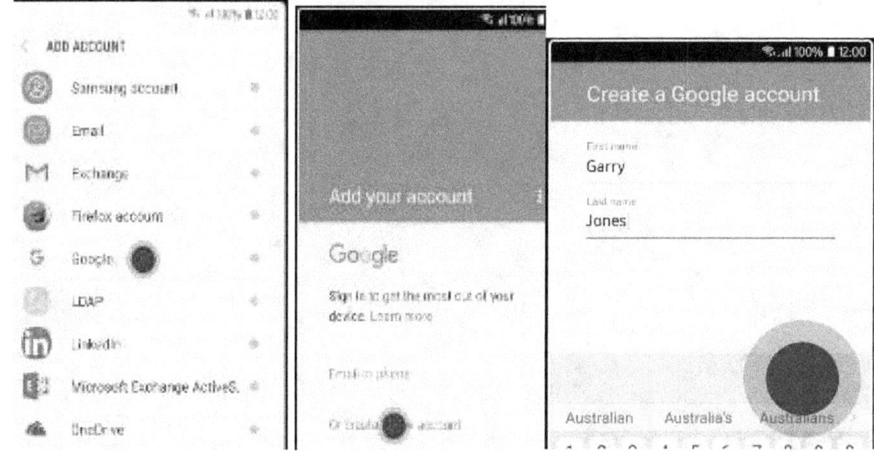

- Next, key in your birthday and gender information and tap **Next**
- Type in your preferred user name and tap **Next**

- Key in a password, confirm it and then tap **Next**

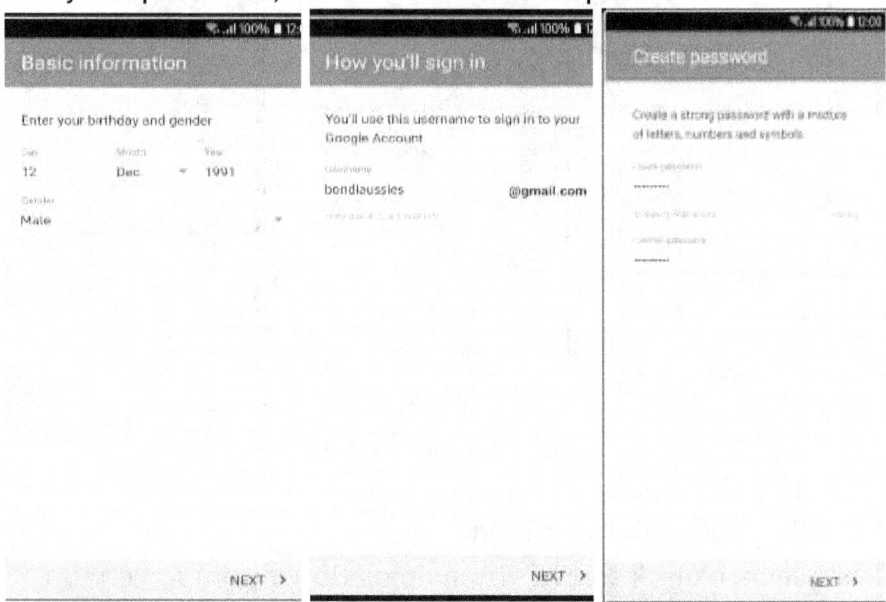

- If needed, enter your phone number and tap **Next**
- Agree to the terms and conditions and tap **Next**
- Finally, confirm your information and tap **Next**

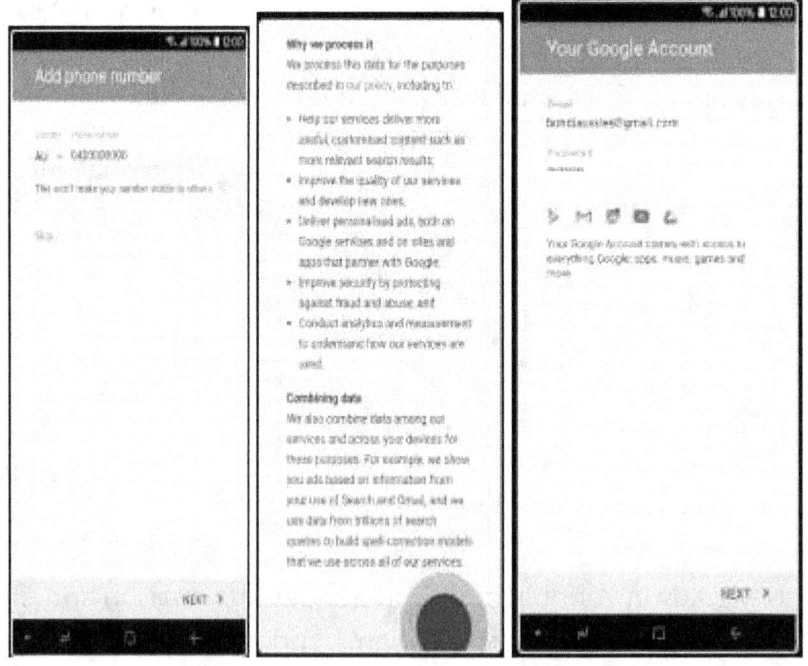

Creating a Samsung account

- Launch quick settings by **swiping down** from screen top
- From **Settings,** select **Cloud and accounts**
- Tap **Account**
- Tap **Add account**

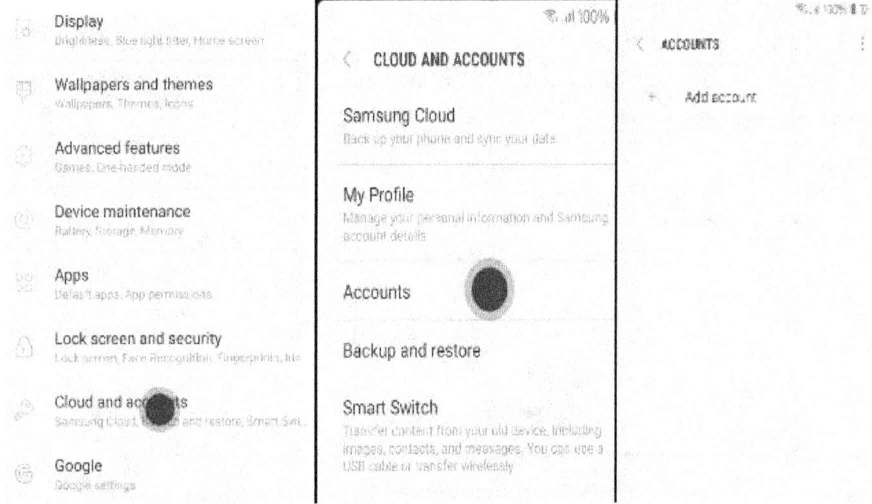

- From the next screen, select **Samsung account** from top of the screen
- Navigate down and select **Create account** at screen bottom left
- Next, fill in the required information and tap **Next**

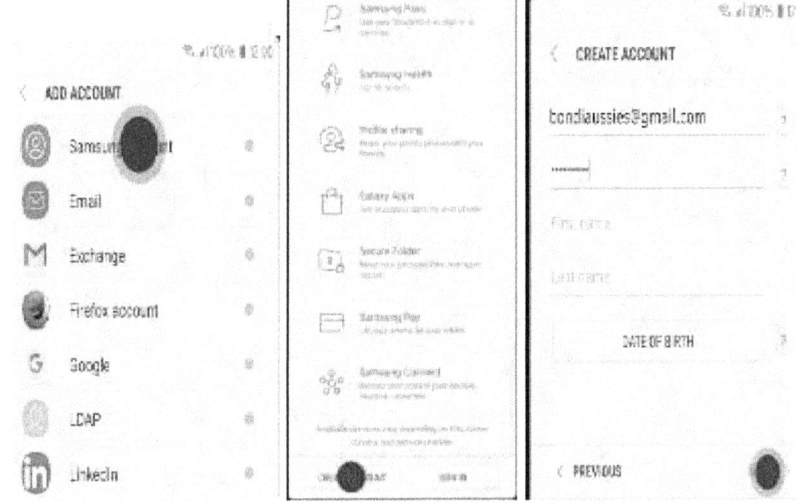

- Agree to the terms and conditions by tapping **"I agree to all"** and then tap **Agree** at bottom right
- Finally, tap **Done** at bottom right

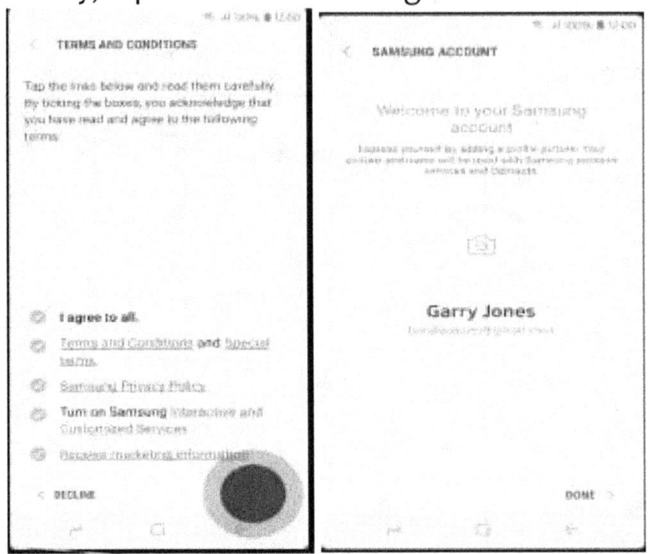

Managing your Samsung account

- Launch **Settings**
- Tap on your name at the top
- Tap **profile info**
- Select the information you want to edit
- Tap **Save** when done

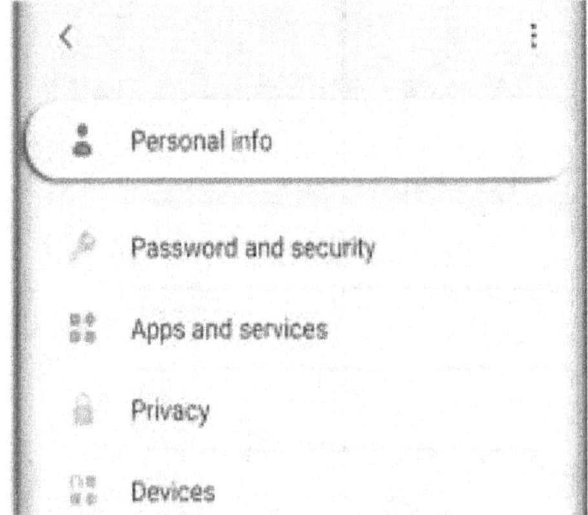

Setting up IMAP email

- Launch quick settings by **swiping down** from screen top
- Tap **Settings**
- Select **Accounts and backup**
- Tap **Manage Accounts**

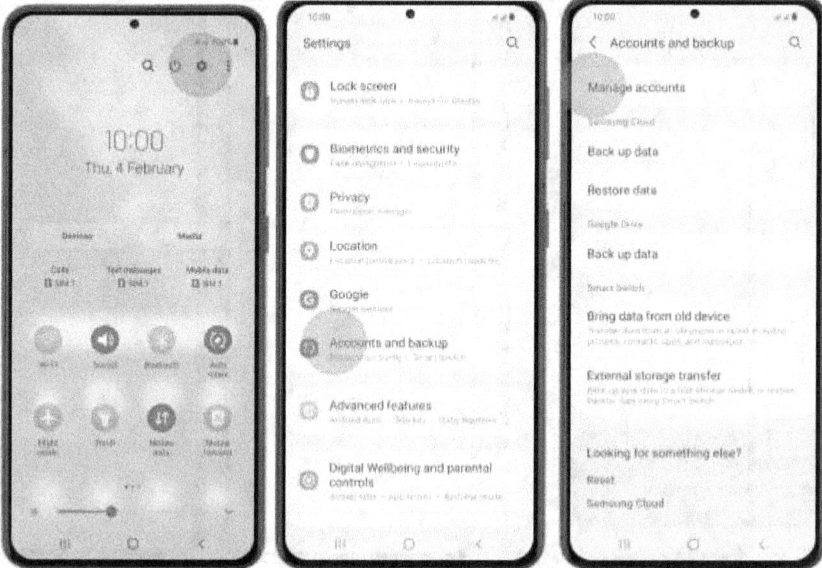

- Tap **Add account**
- Select Personal (IMAP)
- Key in your mail address and tap **Next** at screen bottom

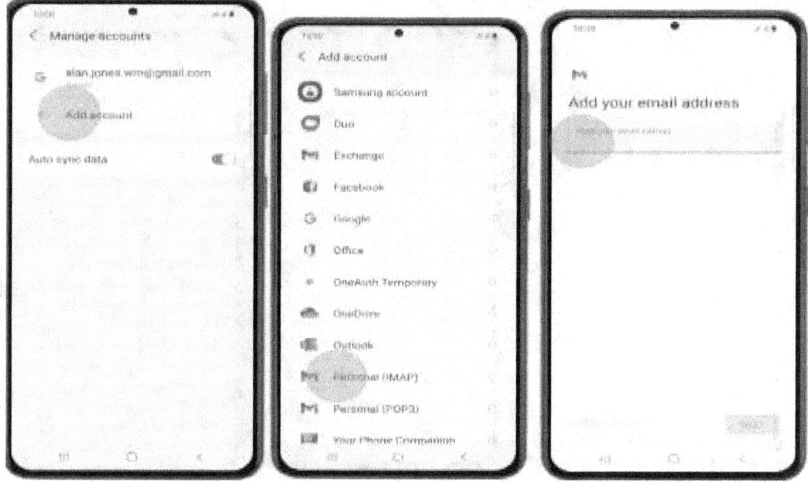

- Key in your password and tap **Next** at screen bottom
- On the account options display, select your preferences and tap **Next** at screen bottom
- On the incoming server settings screen, key in the user name for your email account

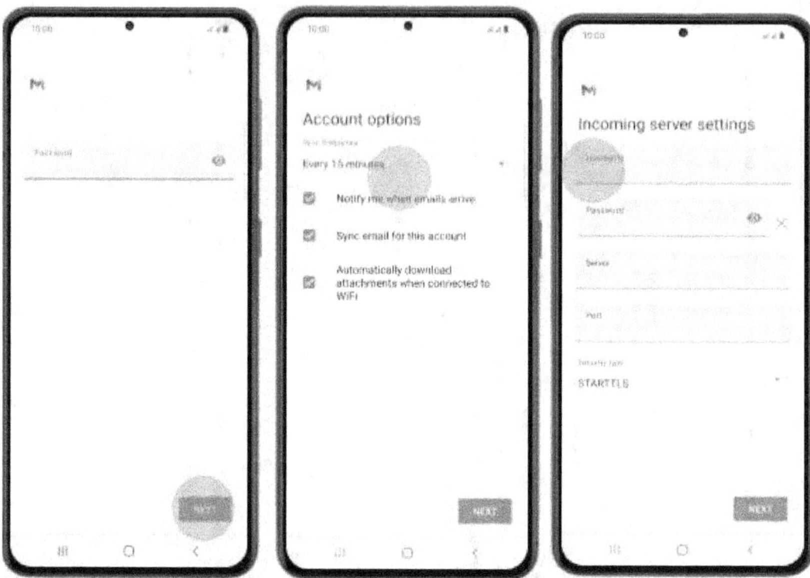

- Next, key in the name of your email provider's incoming server
- In the field below port, enter the numbers 143
- From below security type, call up the dropdown list and select **None** and then tap **Next**

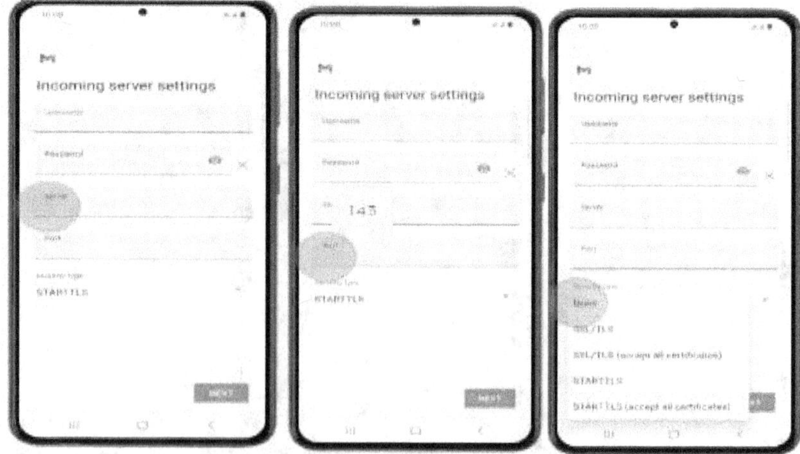

- On the outgoing server settings page, turn on the **"Require sign in"** function
- In the field below username, enter the **name** of your email provider's outgoing server
- In the field below password, enter the **password** of your provider's outgoing server

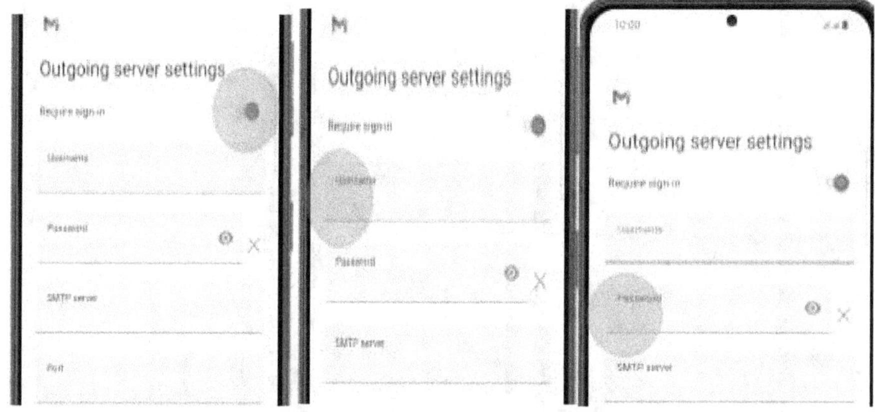

- In the field below SMTP server, enter the **name** of your provider's outgoing server
- In the field below port, enter the number **25**
- Next, from below security type, call up the dropdown list and select **None**

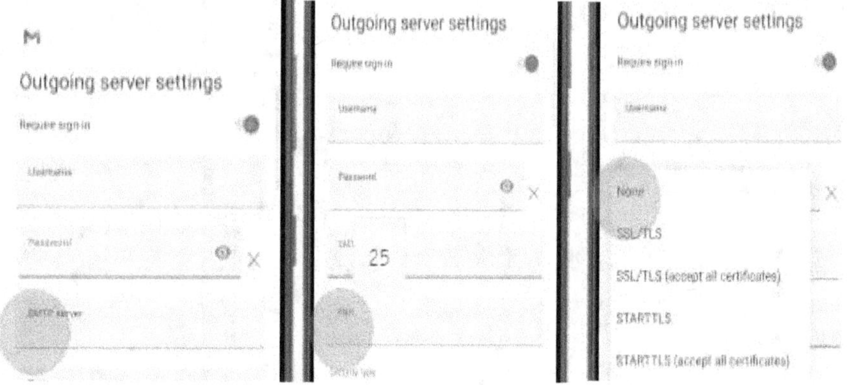

- Tap **Next**
- On the Account options page, specify your preferred settings and tap **Next** at screen bottom

- On the next page, in the field below "Account name (optional)", key in the required name

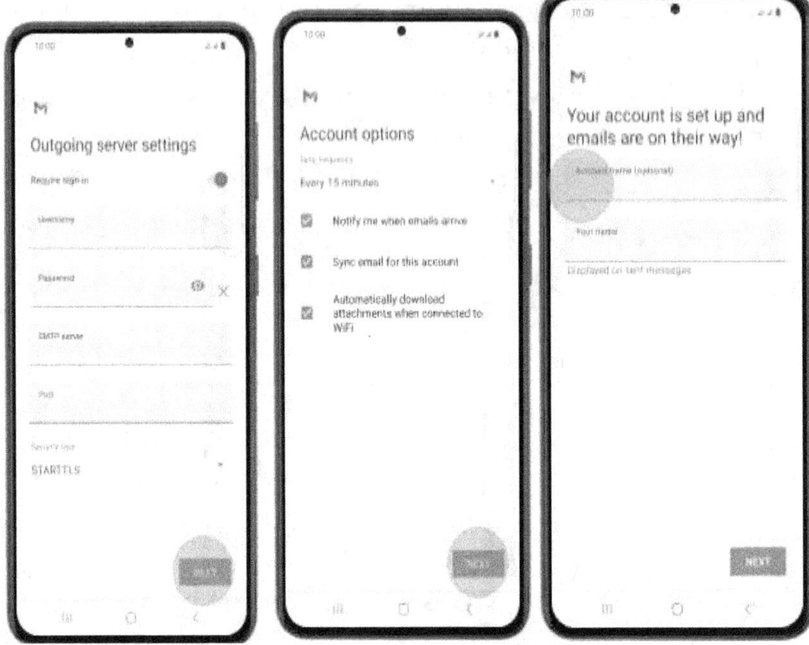

- In the field below **"your name"** enter the required sender name
- Tap **Next**
- Finally, tap the **home key** to go back to the home screen

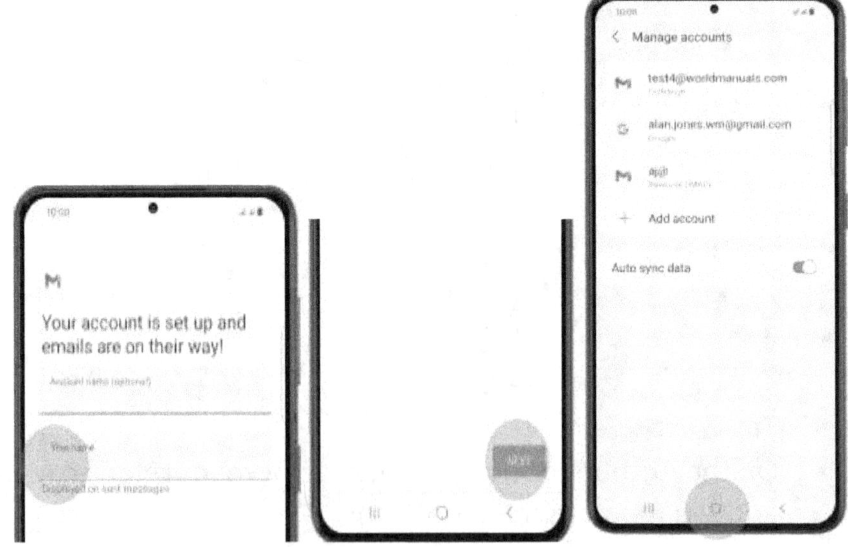

Setting up POP3 Email

- Swipe down from screen to launch the quick settings display
- Tap **settings**
- Tap **Accounts and backup**
- Tap **Manage accounts**
- Tap **Add accounts**
- Select Personal (POP3)
- On the next screen, enter your email address and tap **Next**

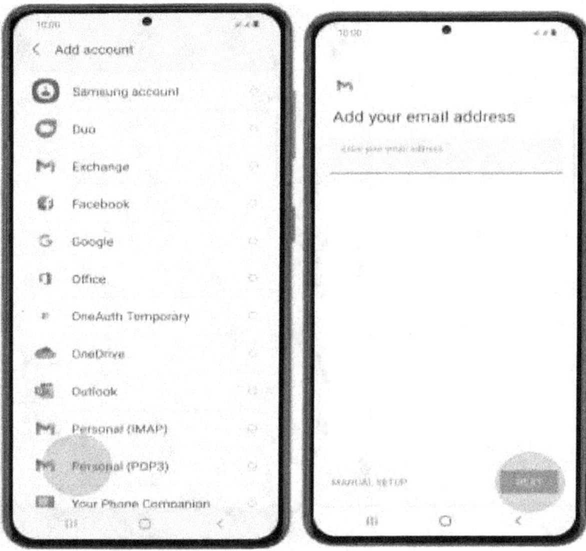

- Key in your password and tap **Next**
- On the **Account options** display, specify your preferred settings
- On the incoming server settings screen, enter following information:
    1. Email account **username**
    2. **Name** of your email provider's incoming server
    3. In the field below "Port", enter the number **110**
    4. Tap the **drop-down list** beside Security type and select **None**
    5. Tap the **drop-down list** beside "Delete emails from server" select an option and tap **Next**

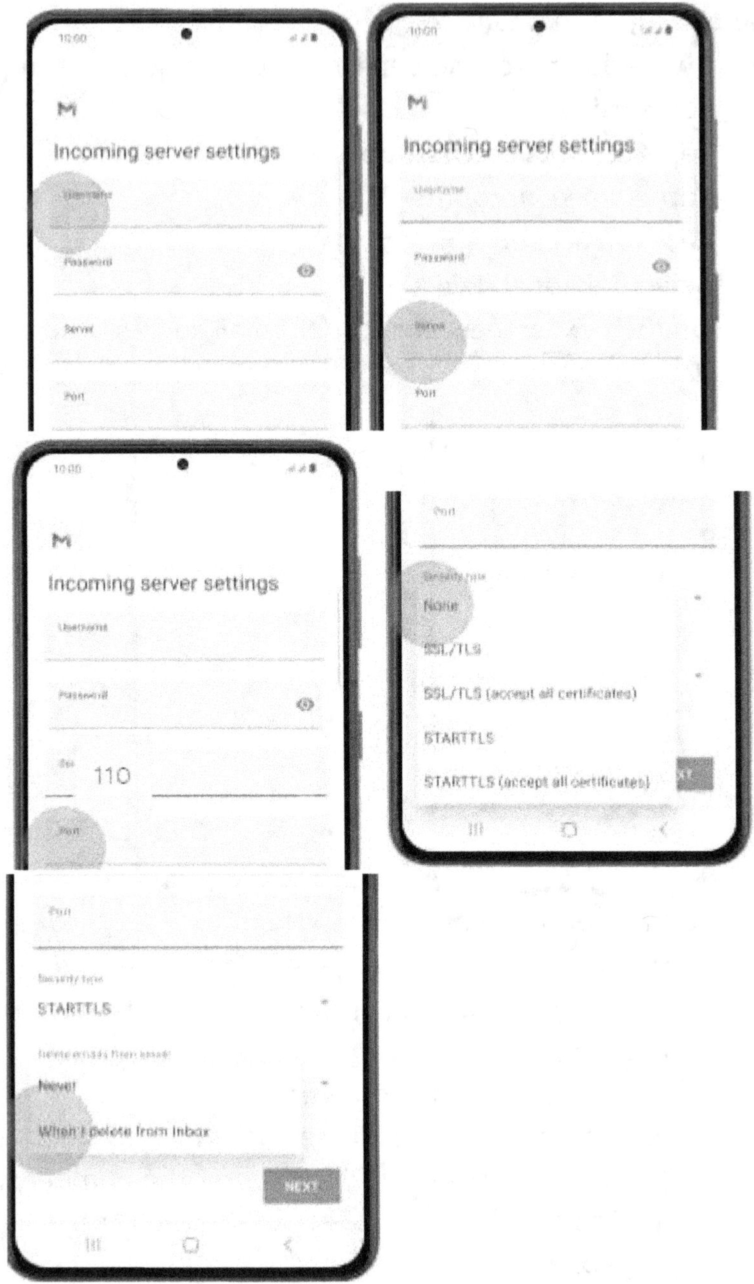

- On the outgoing server settings page, turn on the **"Require sign-in"** function

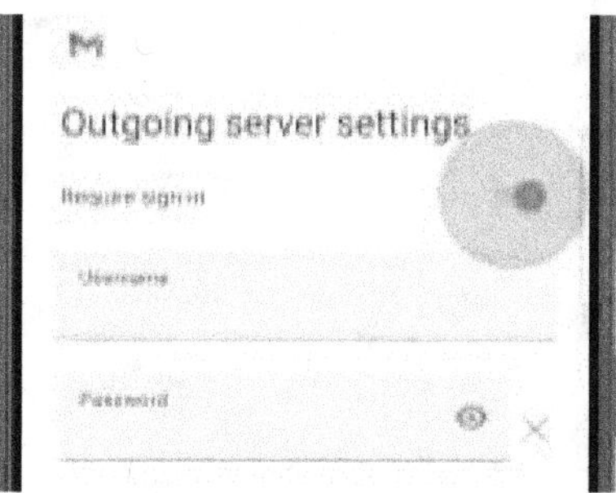

- Next, enter the following information:
    1. Email provider's outgoing server **user name**
    2. **Password** of your provider's outgoing server
    3. In the field below "SMTP server", enter the **name** of your provider's outgoing server
    4. In the field below "Port" enter the number **25**
    5. Call up the **drop-down list** beside "Security type" and select None and tap **Next**

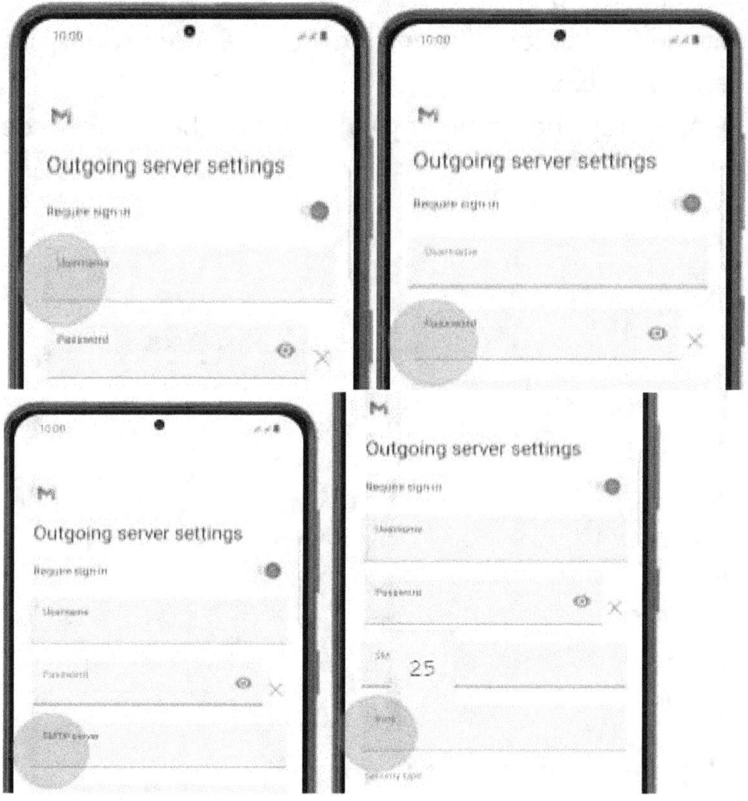

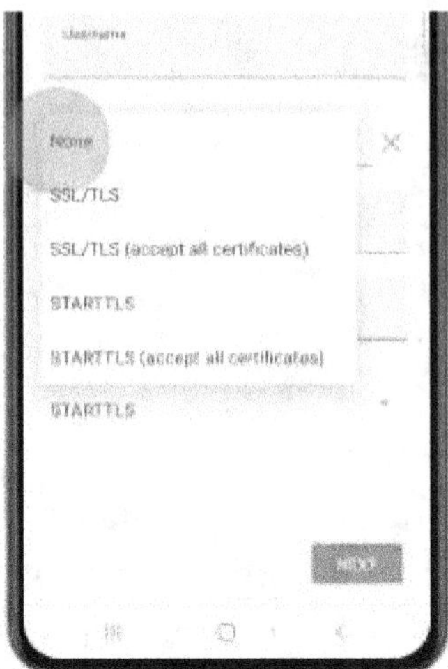

- On the Account options page, specify your preferred options and tap **Next**
- On the next page, below the field **Account name (Optional),** enter the required name
- In the field below **"Your name",** enter the proper sender name and tap **Next**
- Finally, tap the **home key** to return to the home screen

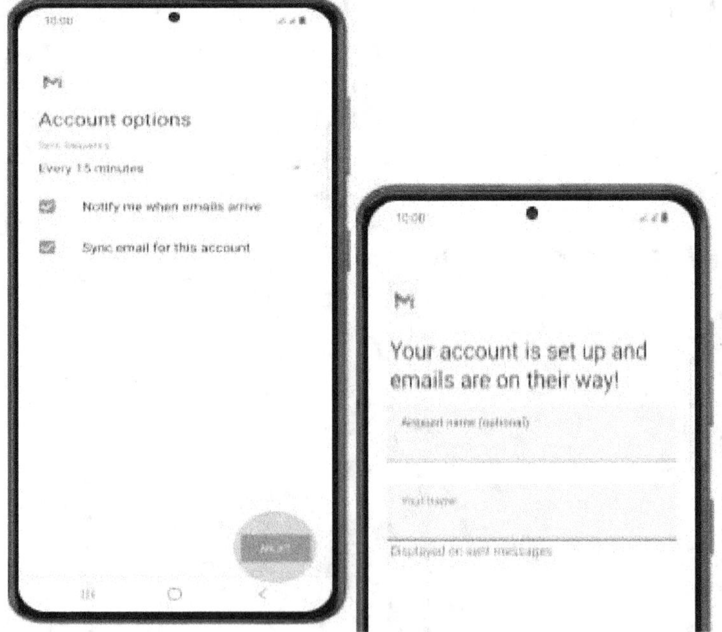

Sending mail

- From screen bottom, **swipe upwards** to open the apps page
- Tap **Google**
- Select **Gmail**
- Tap the email accounts symbol at screen top right

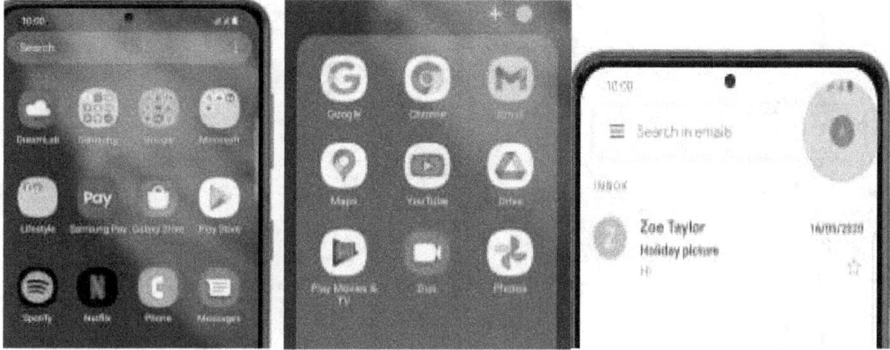

- Choose the required email account
- Tap **Compose** at bottom right of screen
- Enter the recipient's name or email address in the field next to "**To**"

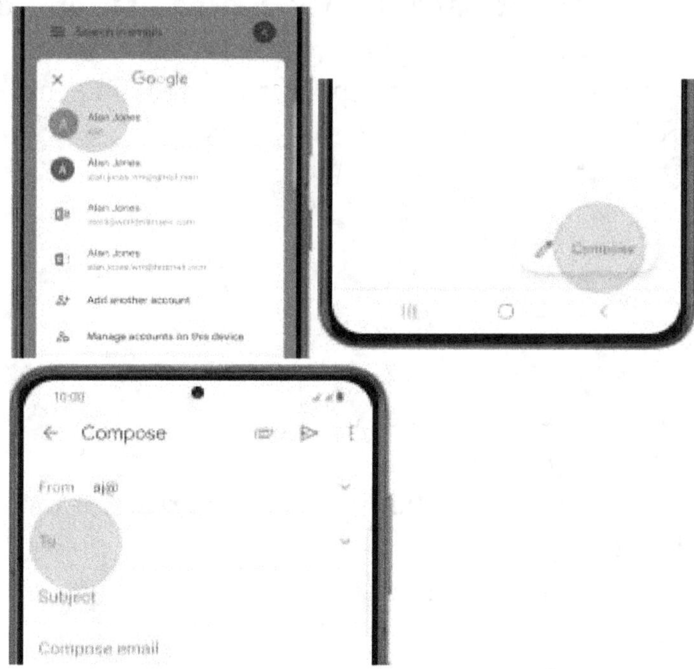

- In the **subject field,** type the email subject

- Next, tap **Compose mail** and type out the email in the text field
- If need be, tap on the attachment icon to attach document,

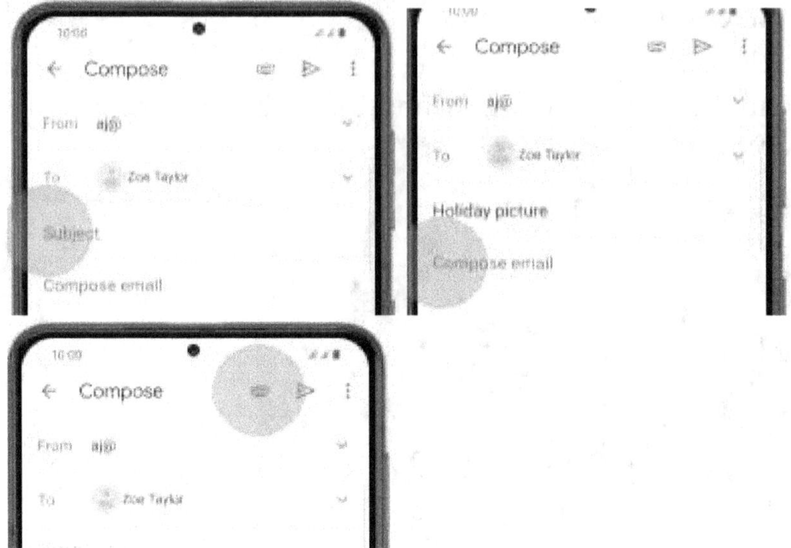

- Tap on **Attach file** and go to the proper folder to select the file or document
- When you have located the file to be attached, **tap on it** to attach it to the email to be sent
- To send the email, tap on the send button or symbol in between the attach symbol and the 3 dots

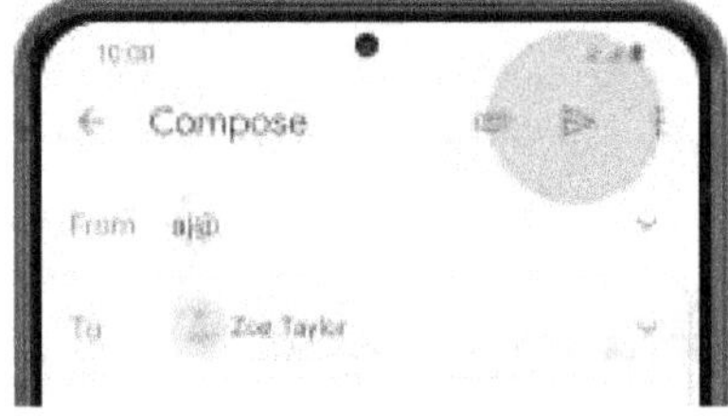

Turning email notifications on or off

- Launch the **email app**
- Tap on the **menu symbol that shows as** 3 horizontal lines stacked vertically
- Next, tap the **Settings** symbol

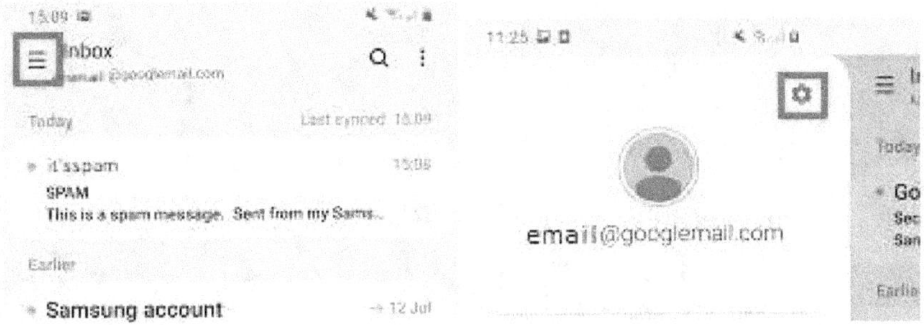

- Select **Notifications**
- Turn notifications on or off by tapping the **indicator** beside Show notifications

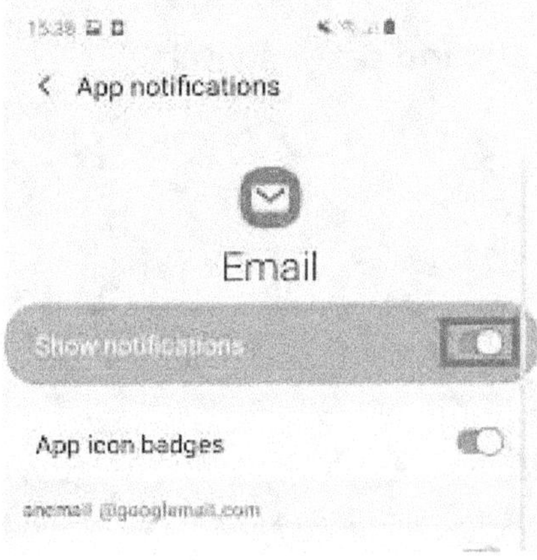

Setting notifications for individual accounts

To do this, you must have the notifications feature activated on your device and you must have more than one email account registered on your device.

- Launch **Notifications**. The account would show at the top as shown below:

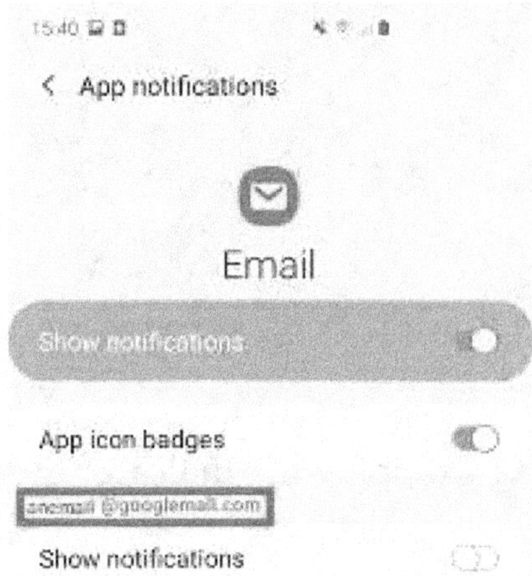

- Select on or off by tapping the **indicator switch**

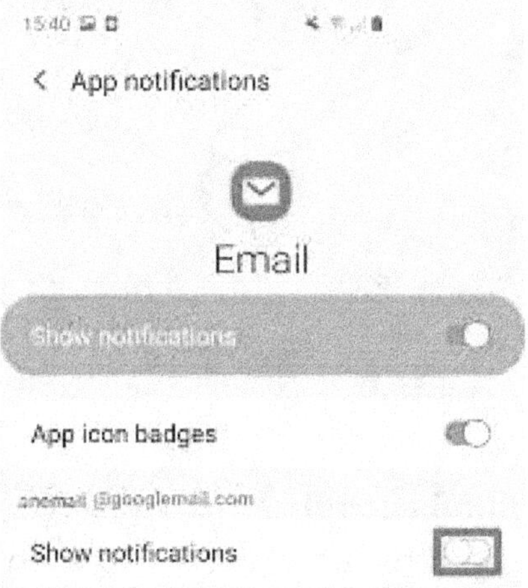

- To access more notifications settings for individual accounts, tap **New emails**
- Specify your preferred settings from the list

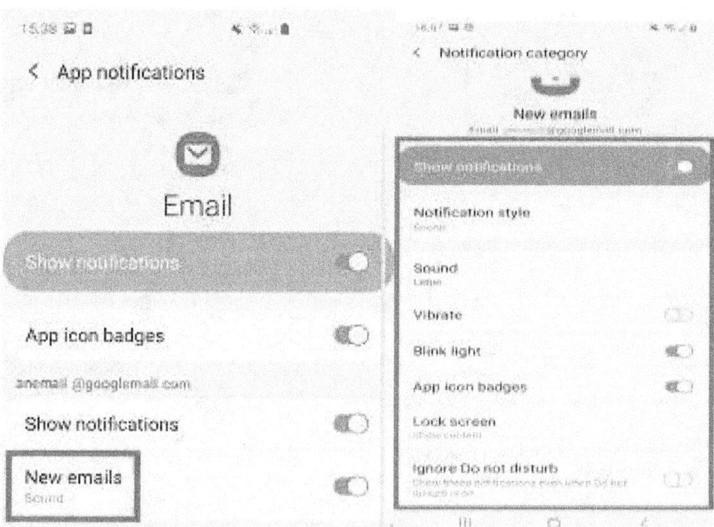

Creating a new email folder

You can use folders to organize your email inbox for better productivity.

- Launch the **email app**
- Tap the **menu symbol**
- Tap **All folders**
- Navigate to the bottom and tap **Create folder**
- Next, select a **location** for your new folder.
- Tap **Root** to situate the folder into your list of folders.
- To place the new folder within an existing one, tap on the intended host folder

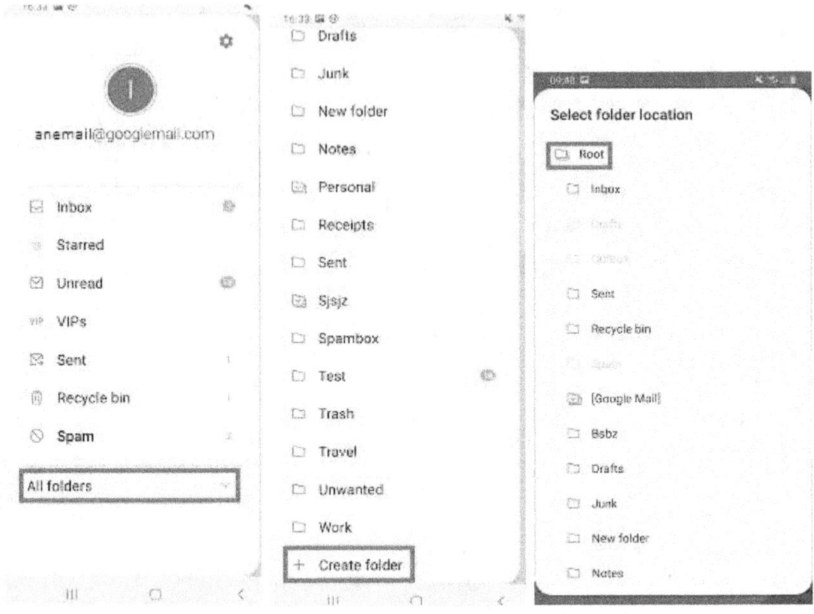

Deleting a folder

- To delete a folder, tap the **menu** icon
- Press and hold the folder to be deleted until a **pop-up** menu shows
- Select **Delete**

Using the find function to locate specific emails

- Launch the **email app**
- Tap the **search symbol** represented as the image of a magnifying glass
- Type a word or phrase in the **search bar**
- You would view all mails that contains the typed word or phrase

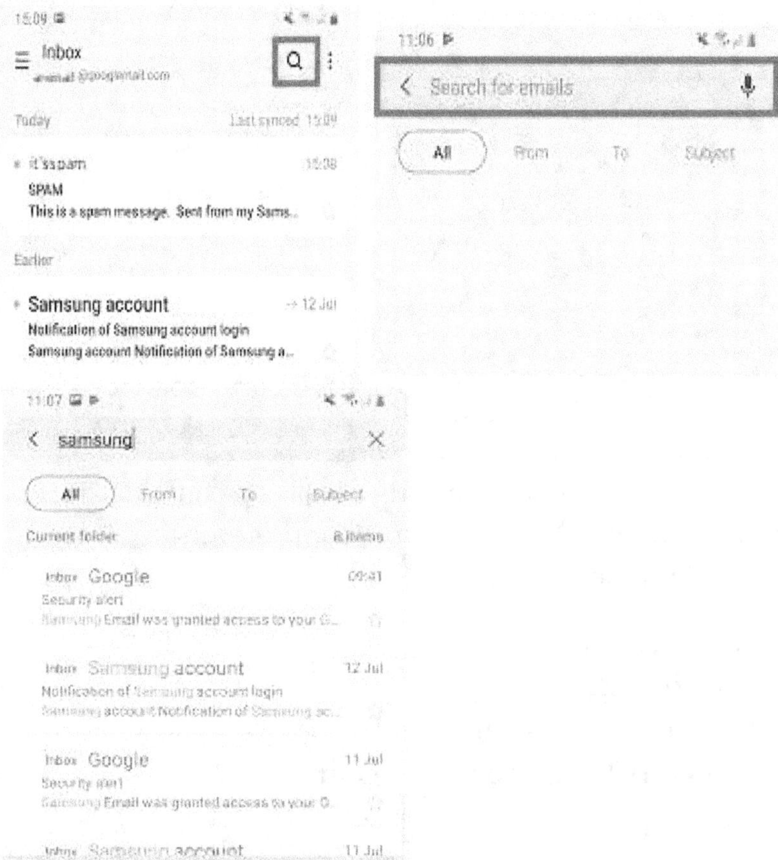

- To find specific mails from a particular contact either sent or received by you, tap **From** or **To**

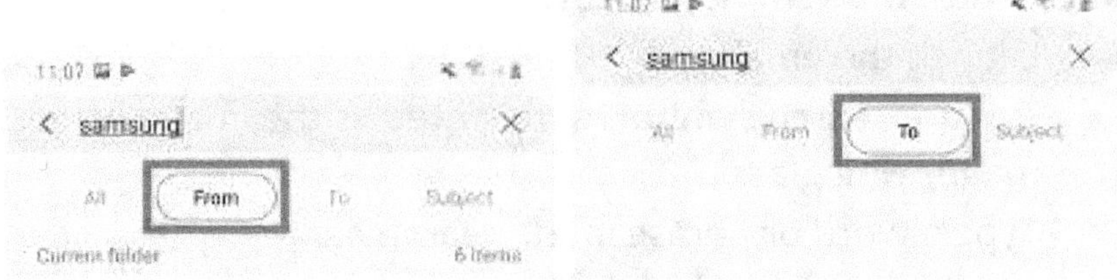

- To locate subject specific emails, tap on **subject**

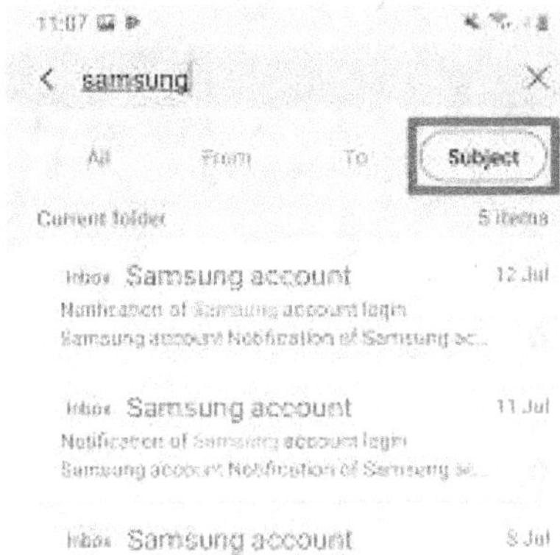

- Tap on a mail when you have found it to open it

Downloading attachments

There are two ways of downloading email attachments. You can do it automatically or manually based on your preference. Whatever be your preference, find the steps below:

- Tap the **Menu symbol**
- Tap **Settings**
- Next, tap an **email account** to edit
- Tap **Auto download attachments**

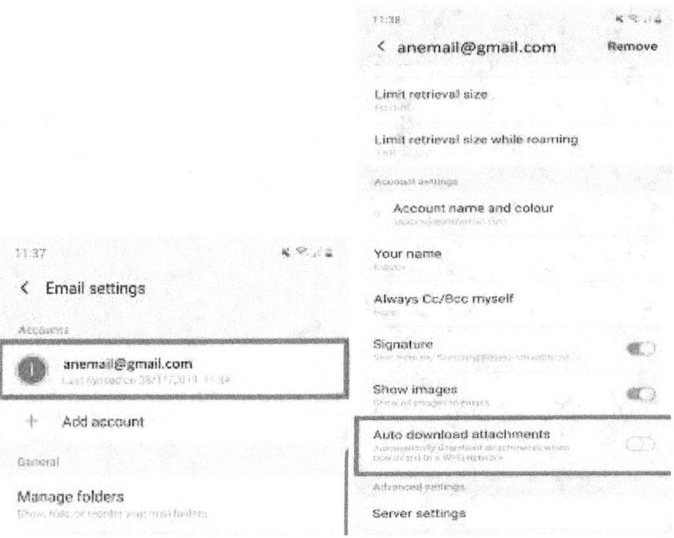

- To do so manually, find an email that has an attachment. Such mail would have a paper clip symbol attached to it
- Tap on the **attachment** or tap **Save** to download it. The attachment would be at the email top
- When the attachment has finished downloading, you would get a prompt to open it with a preferred app. Tap on your **preferred app** to open the attachment when ready

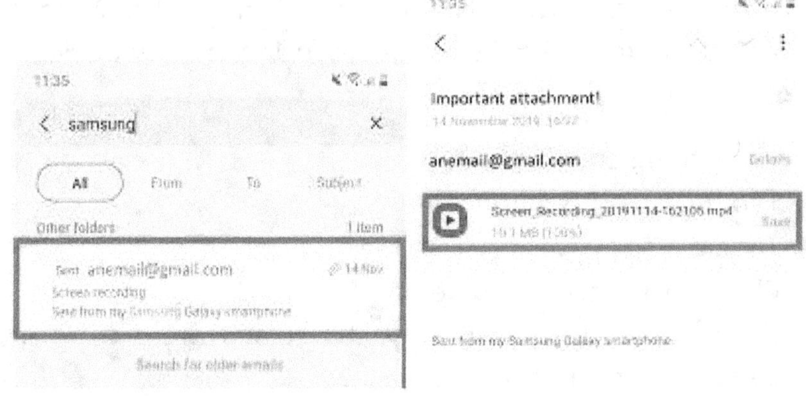

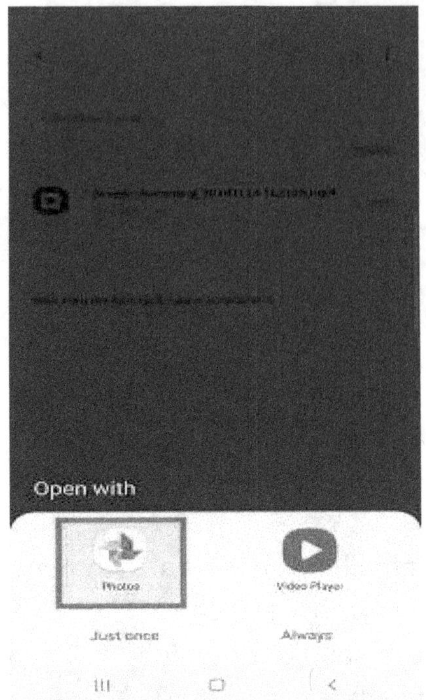

Syncing your mail

You can use the sync function to set emails to automatically download to your Samsung S21, you can equally specify the frequency of the email syncing, which folders would sync and impose a limit on the size of mails to be downloaded. To activate syncing on your device, follow the steps below:

- Launch the **email app**
- Tap the **menu symbol**
- Tap **Settings**
- Choose the account to be synced
- Next, tap the **Sync account switch** to activate syncing and select your preferred settings
- When done, tap the < symbol at top left to go back to your email inbox
- You would now view a display of last synced time at upper right of your screen

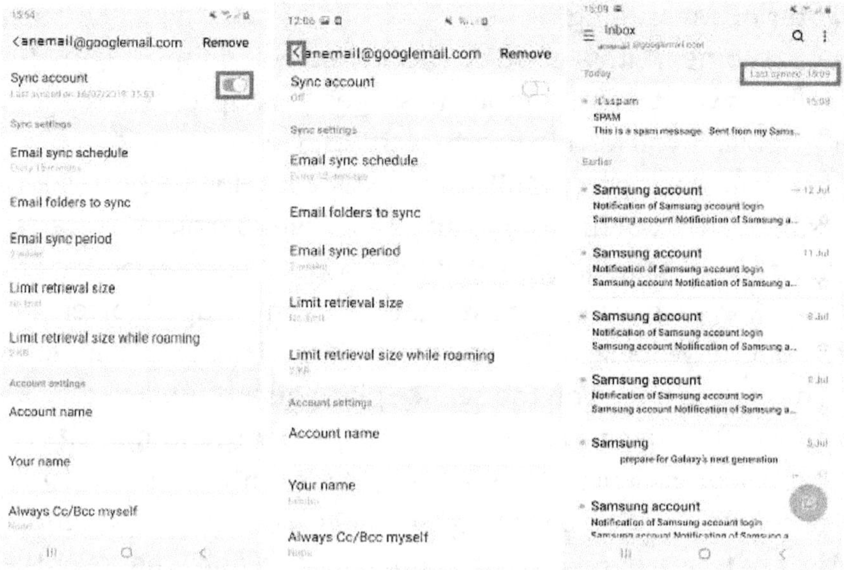

15:54
<anemail@googlemail.com   Remove
Sync account
Last synced on 16/07/2019 15:53
Sync settings
Email sync schedule
Every 15 minutes
Email folders to sync
Email sync period
2 weeks
Limit retrieval size
No limit
Limit retrieval size while roaming
2 KB
Account settings
Account name
Your name
Always Cc/Bcc myself
None

12:06
<anemail@googlemail.com   Remove
Sync account
Off
Sync settings
Email sync schedule
Every 15 minutes
Email folders to sync
Email sync period
2 weeks
Limit retrieval size
No limit
Limit retrieval size while roaming
2 KB
Account settings
Account name
Your name
Always Cc/Bcc myself
None

15:09
Inbox
anemail @googlemail.com
Today
Last synced: 15:09
it's spam
SPAM
This is a spam message. Sent from my Sams...
Earlier
Samsung account   12 Jul
Notification of Samsung account login
Samsung account Notification of Samsung a...
Samsung account   11 Jul
Notification of Samsung account login
Samsung account Notification of Samsung a...
Samsung account   8 Jul
Notification of Samsung account login
Samsung account Notification of Samsung a...
Samsung account   8 Jul
Notification of Samsung account login
Samsung account Notification of Samsung a...
Samsung   5 Jul
prepare for Galaxy's next generation
Samsung account
Notification of Samsung account login
Samsung account Notification of Samsung a...

Chapter 8: Messaging

Your S21 comes with a good old fashioned default messaging function that allows you to send simple messages to recipients with or without multimedia. If you decide to add pictures, video or audio, it becomes a multimedia message or MMS. The text messaging or SMS (short messaging service) function is an alternative to making voice calls or using other messaging apps that work via a Wi-Fi connection and it needs a SIM card inserted to function. Text messaging often works with your network service provider and you are charged as you send text messages based on the service plan you are subscribed to. You can always use this function to send quick or urgent messages to any contact on your device especially when it's not convenient to do a voice communication by calling a contact. You could also send messages to a group with the text messaging app whenever the need arises.

Setting up your phone for messaging

Normally, once you have inserted a SIM into your phone, you should be able to send and receive text messages or SMS and MMS but in case you are not able to do so, you may have to manually set up your S21 for messaging. To do this, find the steps below:

- Go to the apps display by **swiping upwards** on your screen
- Open the message center by tapping **Samsung**
- Tap on **Messages**
- Press the **Menu symbol**

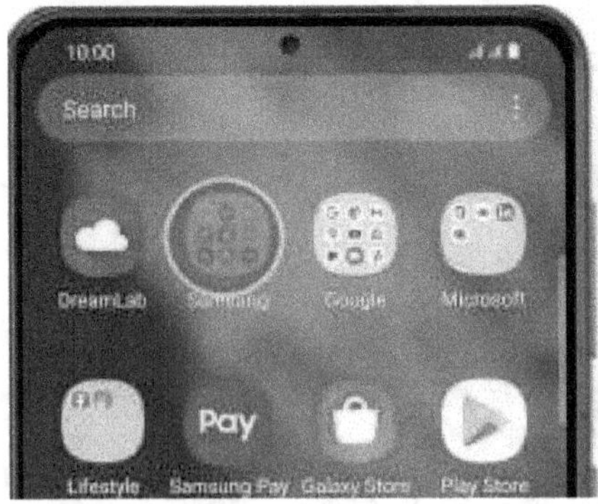
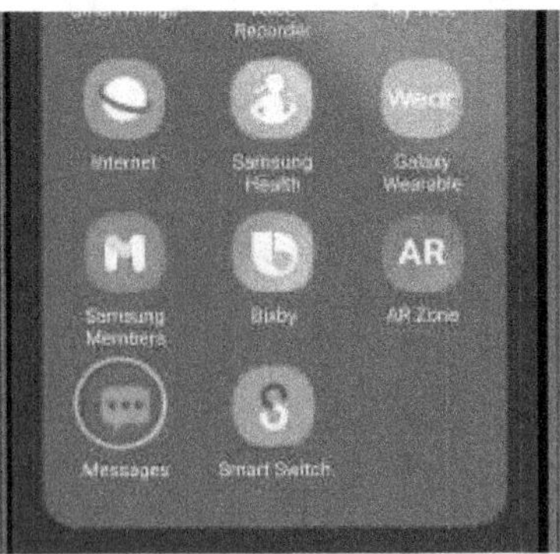

- Tap **Settings**
- Tap **More Settings**
- Select **Text messages**

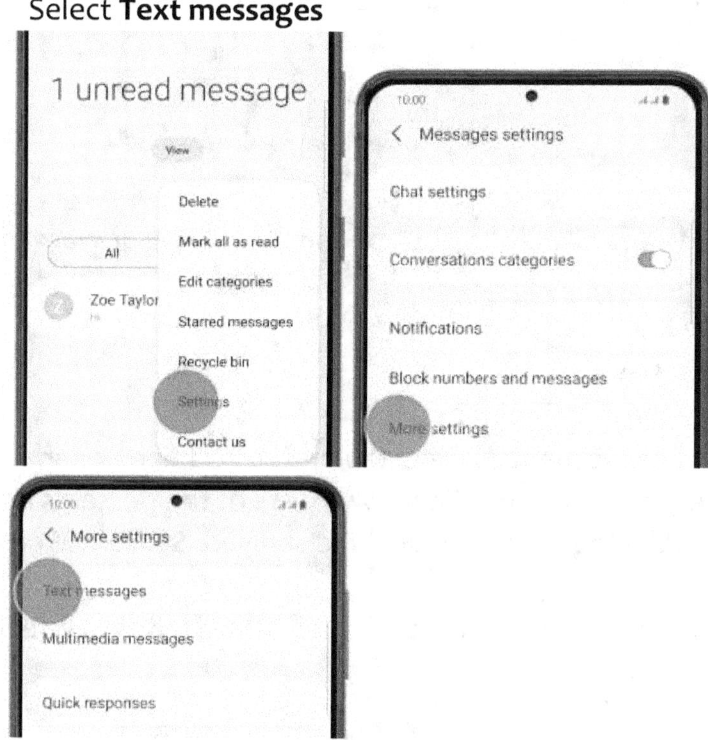

- Next, tap **Message center**
- Key in the **message center number**
- Return to home screen when done

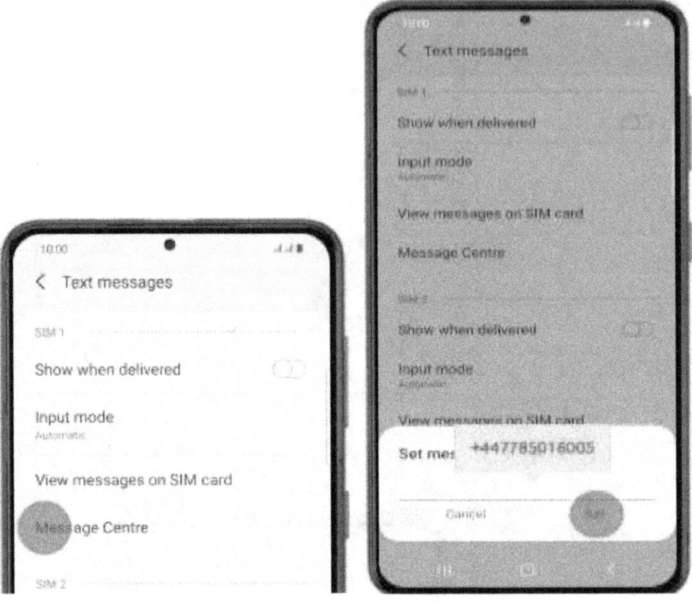

Writing and sending text messages

- Go to the apps display on your phone by swiping upwards on your screen
- Tap **Samsung**
- Tap **Messages**
- Next, tap the **new message symbol**
- To enter the recipient's name, tap on the **recipient's name input field** and enter the first few letters of the person's name. a list of matching names would be displayed. Select the proper one.
- In case you have two SIMs, tap on the **SIM symbol** to select the required SIM

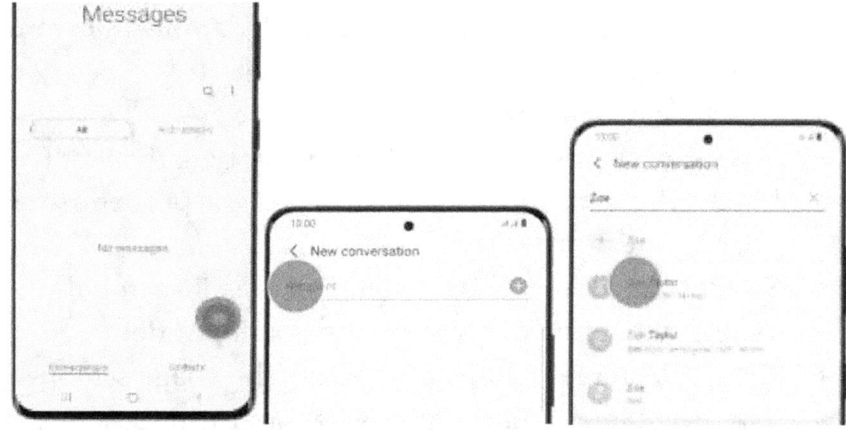

- Tap on the **text input field** and type the message to be sent
- When you have finished typing, press the **send button** to send the text message
- Press the **home button** to return to the home screen

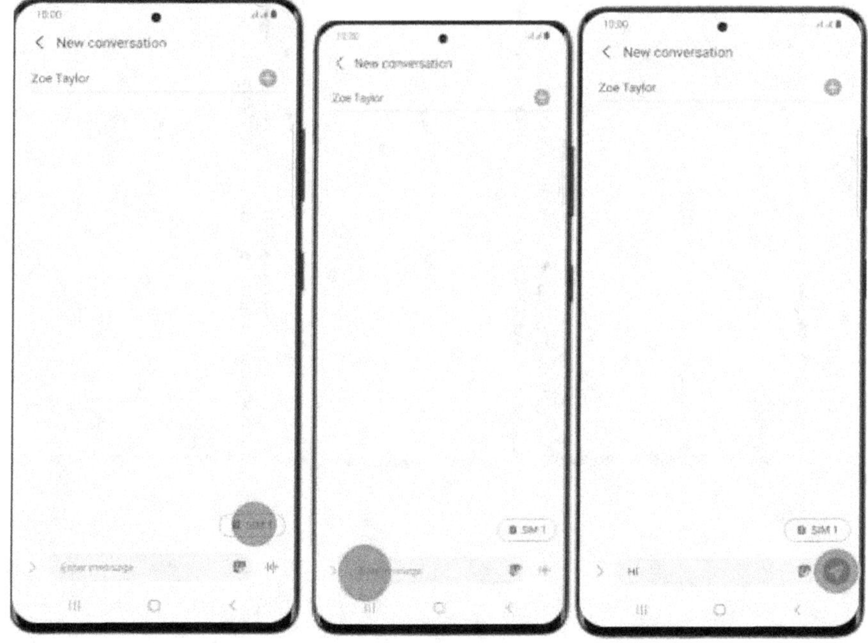

Sending an MMS

An MMS can contain an image, video or an audio clip or a combination of one or two of them. It's an advanced form of the SMS. Find how to create and send an MMS as follows:

- Launch the apps page on your phone by **swiping upwards**
- Tap **Messages**
- Tap the **new message symbol**
- In the **recipient's name text input field**, type the first few letters of the person's name and select the proper name from the list that would show
- Select the proper SIM by tapping on the **SIM symbol**
- Type the text for your MMS in the **text input field**
- Next, tap on the **right arrow** and tap the image symbol
- Tap the **gallery symbol** and navigate to the necessary folder
- Select the desired picture

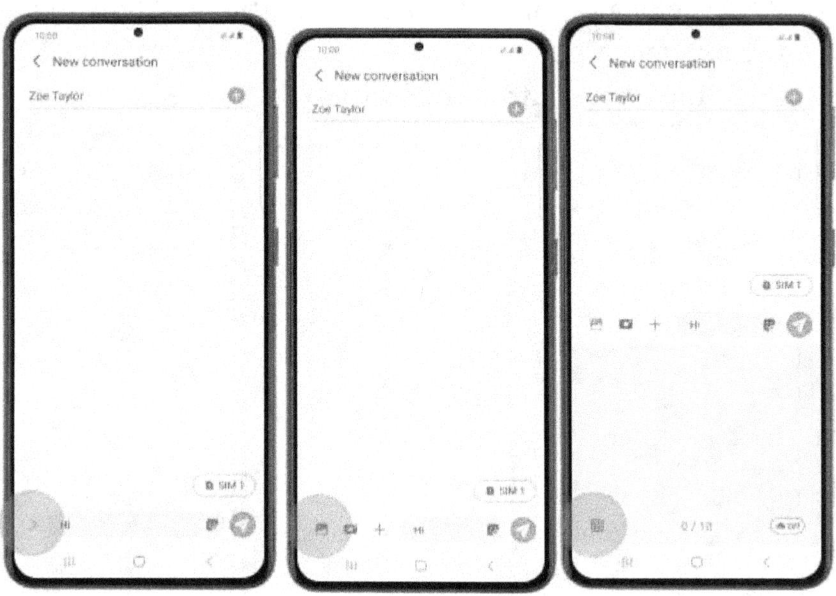

- Tap **Done**
- Tap the **send symbol** to send MMS when you are through
- Tap the **home key** to return to the home screen

Viewing new messages

- To use the notifications panel to view new messages, **swipe down** from screen top and then tap the **New message notification**
- To view new messages from the messaging app, just launch the **messaging app** and then tap on the **conversation** with the new message
- To hear and view an MMS message attachment, tap **Play**

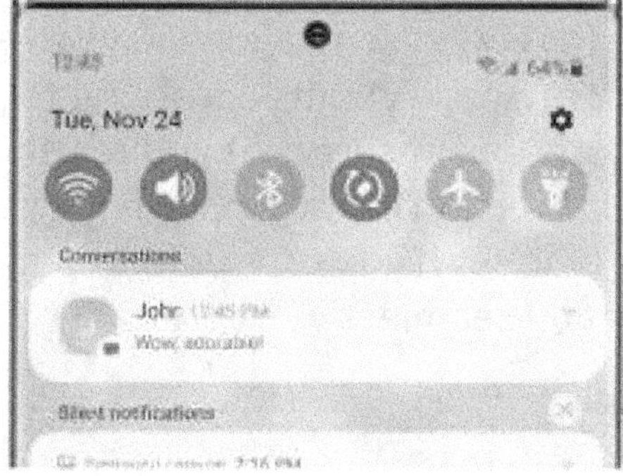

Deleting messages

- Launch the **messaging app**
- Tap the **Conversations tab**
- Press and hold the message to be deleted
- Next, tap **Delete** at screen bottom
- Tap **Move to trash** to confirm

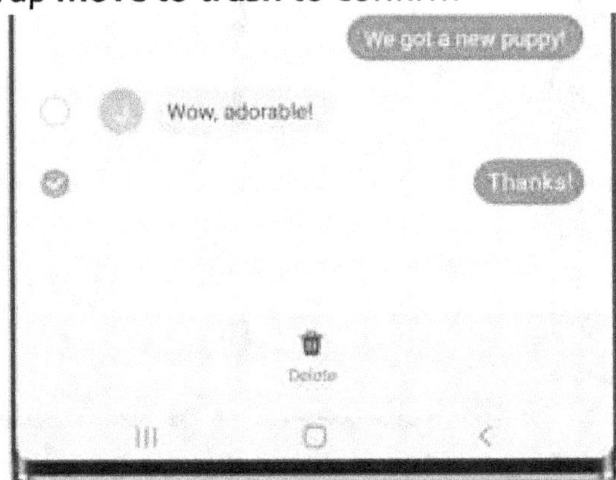

Recovering deleted messages

- From the messaging app, tap **More options** shown by 3 vertical dots
- Tap **Trash**
- Next, **tap and hold** the message to be recovered
- Tap **Restore**

Dual messenger

The dual messenger grants you the capability and flexibility of having two separate accounts for one single messaging app. when you set up this feature, it would be possible for you to send and receive messages to or from any one of the two active App accounts according to your preference. To use both versions of App, ensure that you're using separate credentials on the second version of the App. No matter the purpose or application: for work or leisure, you can run the same app for two different accounts faster and seamlessly.

Setting up Dual messenger

- Launch **Settings**

- Go to **Advanced features**
- Navigate down and tap on **Dual messenger**

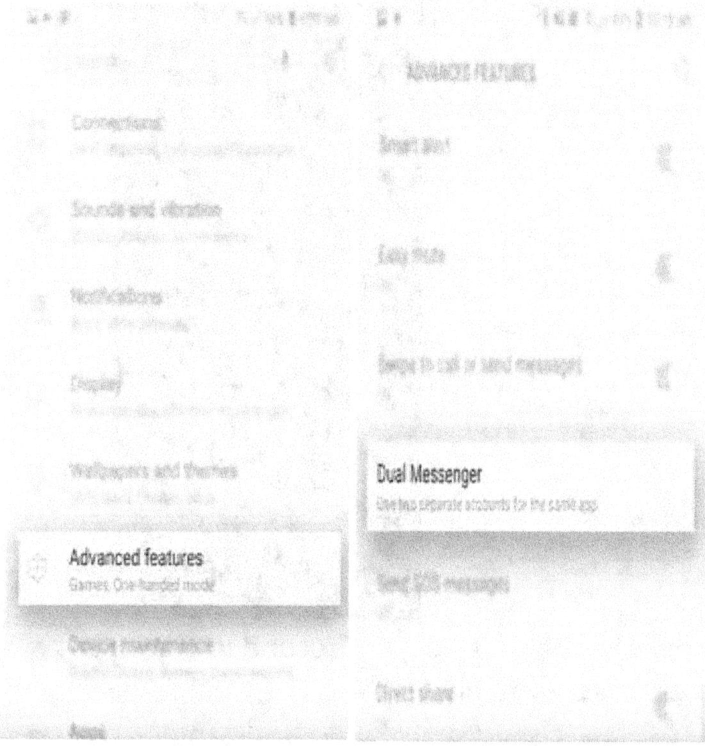

- From the displayed list of apps compatible with dual messenger, select the one you want to have a separate account for by turning the **switch** on

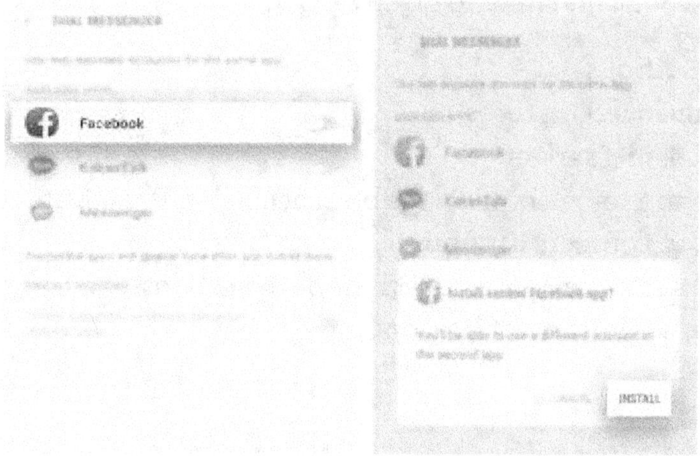

- Next, tap **Install**
- View the disclaimer and tap **Confirm**

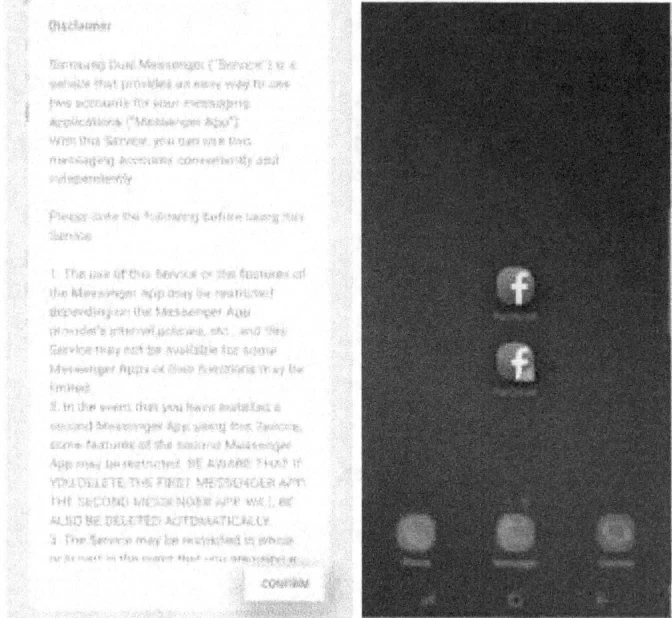

- On its right lower right side, the second icon would have the dual messenger symbol

Dual messenger contact settings

When you set up dual messenger, you have the option of deciding to use the same contacts or separate contacts for both accounts. Whichever one it is, find how to do so below:

- Go to **Settings**
- Tap **Advanced features**
- Tap **Dual messenger**
- To use the same contacts for both accounts, deactivate the **Use separate contacts list** option
- To use separate contacts lists for both accounts, activate the **Use separate contact lists** option

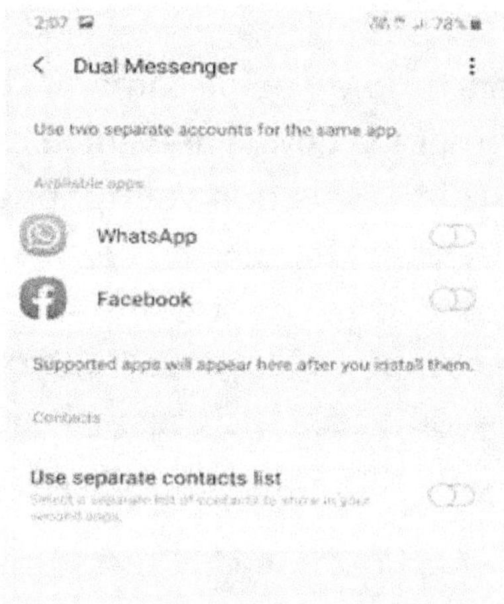

Message settings

- From within the messaging app, tap **More options** represented by 3 vertical dots
- Tap **Settings** and then make your preferred adjustments

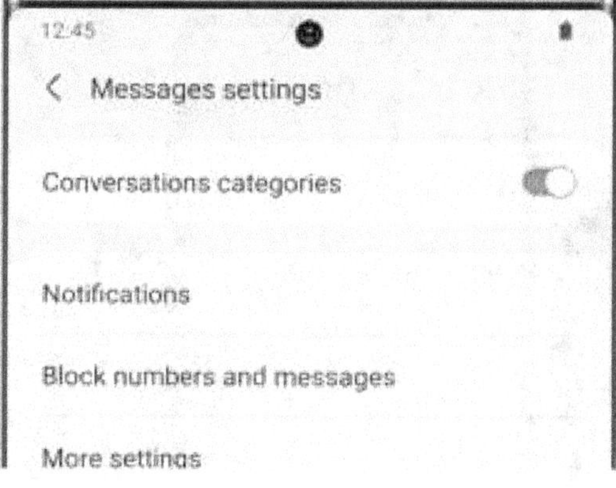

Chapter 9: Camera

Your S21 comes with 3 rear cameras and a 10MP selfie camera. The rear cameras include a 64MP telephoto camera, a 12MP wide angle camera and a 12MP ultra wide-angle camera. This means that your phone has a highly capable camera that you can use to take breathtaking shots and capture anything that catches your fancy. In case you are into photography, the camera has quite a number of settings that you can use to tweak your images and create world class pictures. To know how to use and get the best from the camera, follow the steps below:

Launching the camera

- To launch the camera, you have three options:
    1. you can swipe up from home screen to go to your apps page and then tap on the **Camera app**
    2. you can launch the camera from the lock screen by simply **swiping** the camera symbol upwards
    3. you can also do it via the quick launch feature by **double tapping** the side key in quick succession

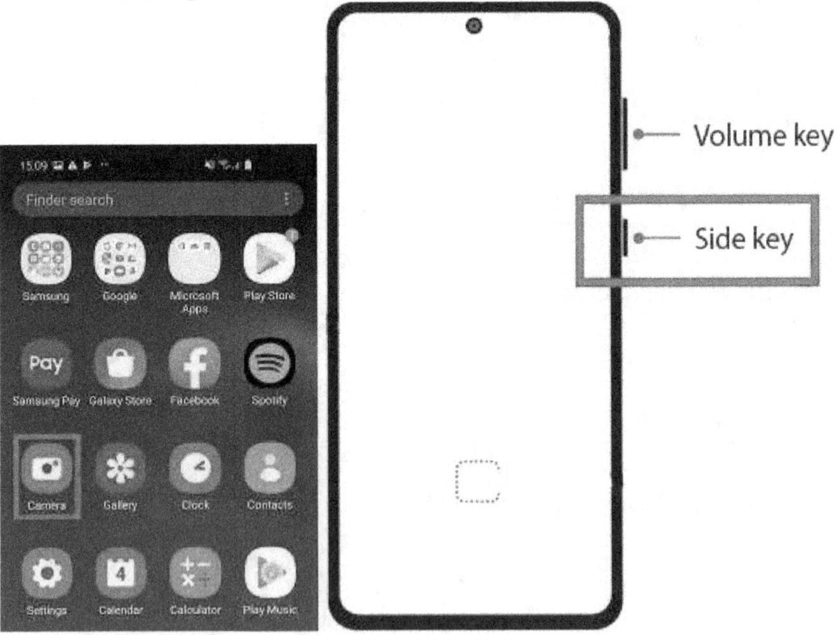

By default, the quick launch feature of the side key is set to launch the camera but in case you assign it to another app for e.g, Bixby or some other app, you would have to re-assign it to launch the camera. To do so, follow steps below:

- to enable the camera quick launch feature, go to **Settings**
- next, tap **Advanced features**
- select **Side Key**
- tap **Quick launch camera**

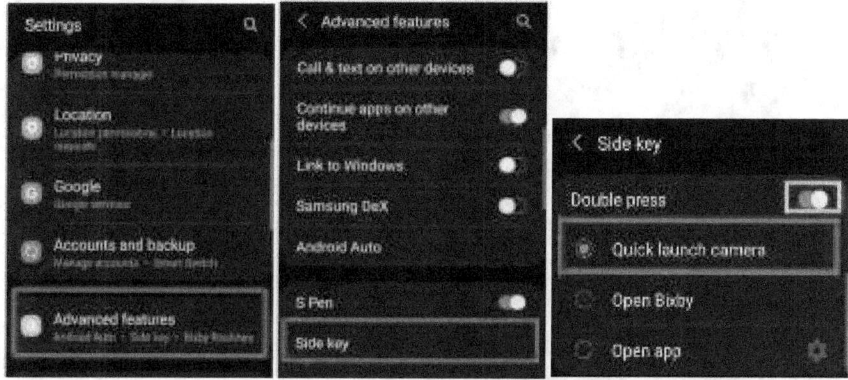

- Another option to access the side key settings is to **press and hold** the side key for about 2-5 seconds. This would call up the power off menu
- from the power off menu, you can tap on **side key settings** at screen bottom and you would be able to do the changes shown above

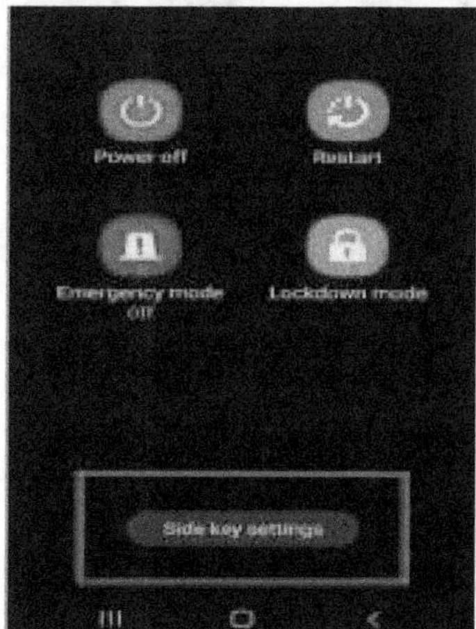

Taking a picture

- with the camera app open, just point the phone at any image you want to capture and tap the **shutter button**

Recording a video

- with the camera app open, tap and hold the shutter button to commence the recording or swipe left and then tap on the record button to start

- when you are done recording, tap the stop recording button

Switching between front and rear cameras

- with the camera app open, tap the **camera switch** button to alternate between both cameras

Zooming in and out

- with the camera app open, touch the screen in two places and then spread both fingers apart to zoom in. To zoom out, repeat the process in reverse

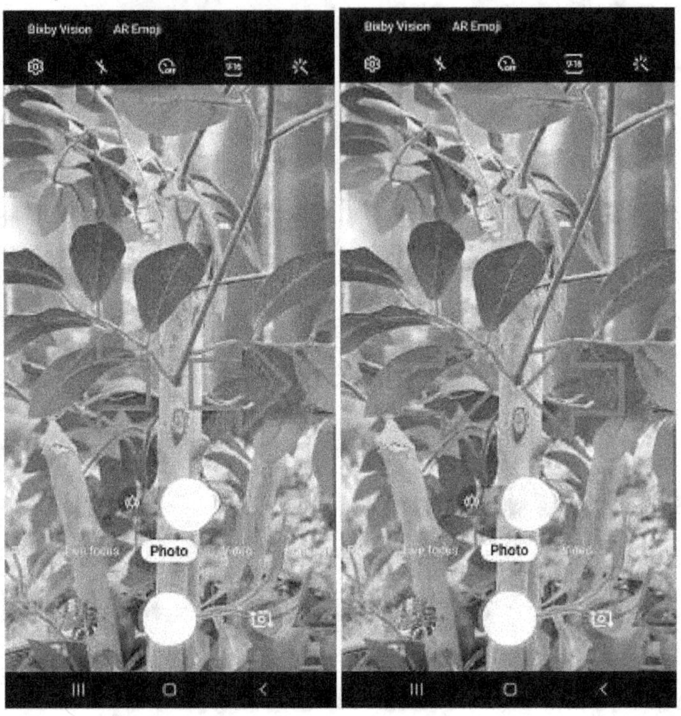

Activating or deactivating the flash

- with the camera app open, locate the **flash symbol** near top of the screen, next to the settings symbol and tap on it. You can set it to on, off or auto.
- To turn on the flash tap on the symbol till it turns yellow. To turn the flash off, do the same in reverse

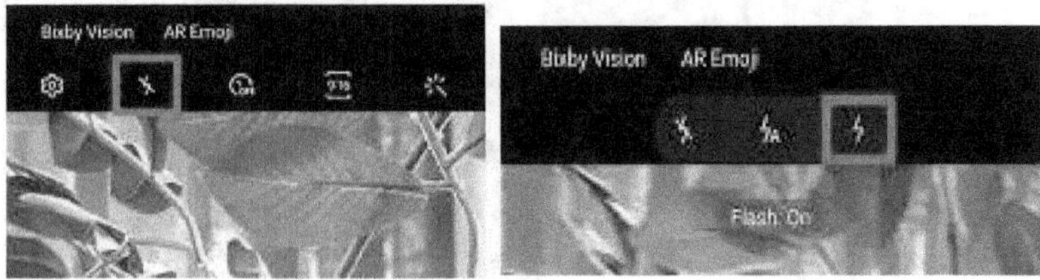

Using the 8k video snap feature

This feature allows you to create images from recorded videos. Follow the steps below:

- Launch the **camera app** and switch to video mode
- Select **8k /24** in the video resolution section
- Record a video of your interest
- Next, access the video from your gallery, play it back and pause it at a desired point
- From the **video playback bar**, select the best single image
- Tap the **screen shot symbol** at upper left and the 8k photo should show up in your gallery

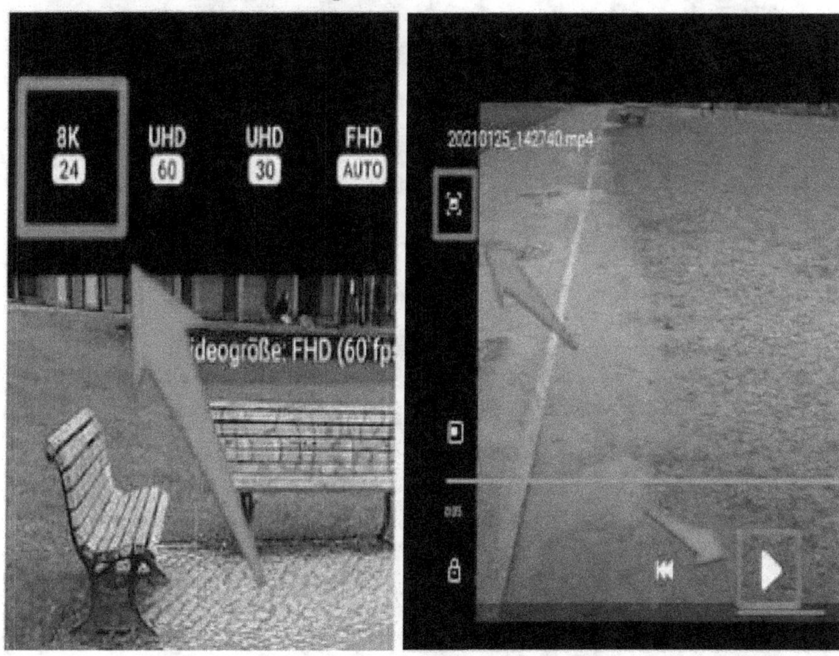

Using the single take camera feature

The "Single Take" mode, allows you to record images with different focal lengths and videos at different speeds simultaneously. This means that you can shoot a subject for a maximum of 15 seconds, then change the angle and wait a bit as the images are processed. From the Gallery app, you would be able to pick from a selection of images and videos that were created from Single Take. To use this feature, follow the steps itemized below:

- From the camera app, select the **Single take** menu item
- Next, specify the desired length of the shot
- You can also select the modes you want activated while capturing single takes
- Record a video of a maximum of 15 seconds

- From the gallery, go to **Single take** and select one of the photos or videos

Using the director's view camera feature

This function allows you to view live viewfinder images from all cameras at the same time. You can equally record selfie videos and main camera footage simultaneously. To use this feature, do the following:

- From the camera app, access the **More menu**
- Next, tap on **Director's view**
- From screen right side, you would now be able to view a live preview of all cameras

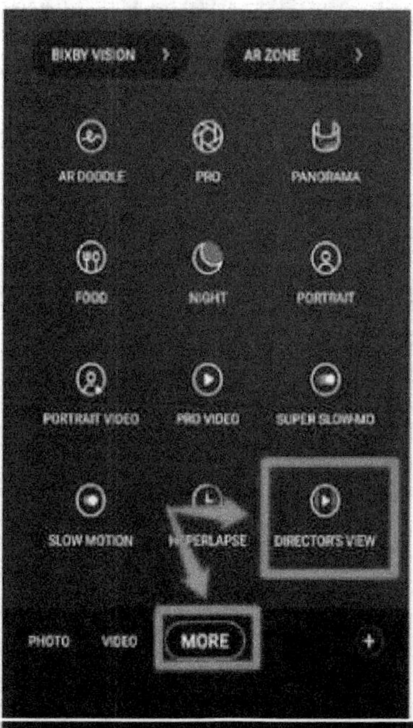

- The symbol in view at top left side of the screen allows you to specify how the selfie image is shown

Zoom lock camera feature

The new zoom lock feature of the s21 allows you to focus on points of interest in a unique way that all but eliminates any kind of shaking. To use this feature, do the following:

- From the image preview screen, **swipe down** on the zoom selection to view the space zoom feature
- Next, focus on the object of interest and tap on the display for a second
- The object of interest should remain centered and stabilized

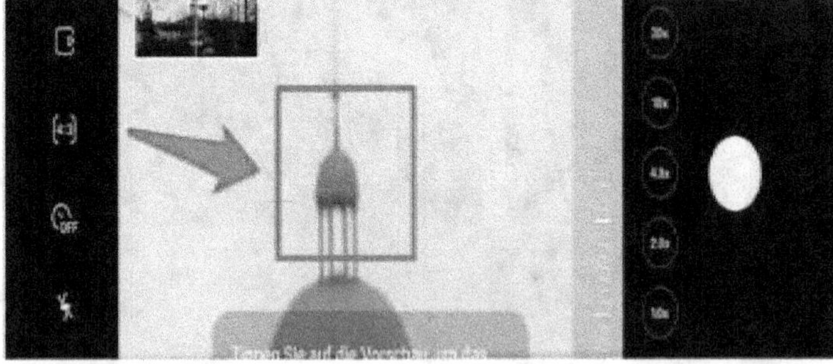

Saving images in HEIF (high efficiency image formats)

This allows you to conserve storage space on your device by converting and storing captured images and videos in smaller formats than the normal JPG format.

- Go to the camera settings
- Select **Format and advanced options**

- Activate the switch for **HEIF pictures**

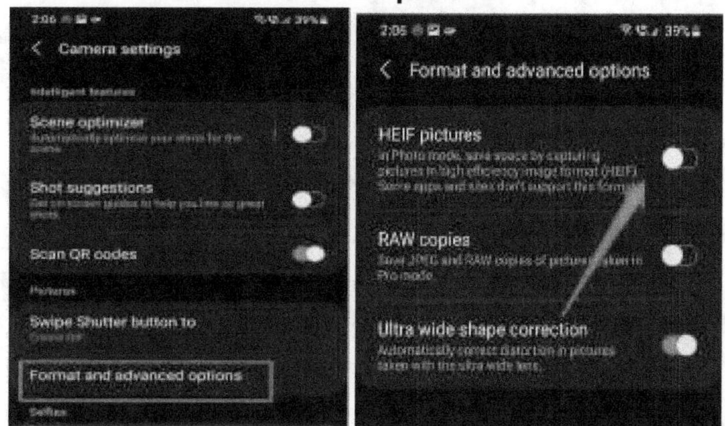

- Do the same for video mode

Turning on HDR 10+ Recording

 HDR10+ allows the camera to capture an increased color range, thereby making your videos more dynamic. It's great for capturing photos and video playback. To activate this function, do the following:

- Launch the camera app
- Switch to video mode
- Tap **Resolution** and ensure that it's set to FHD
- Next, tap **Settings**
- Select **Advanced recording options**
- Activate the switch next to HDR10+ videos

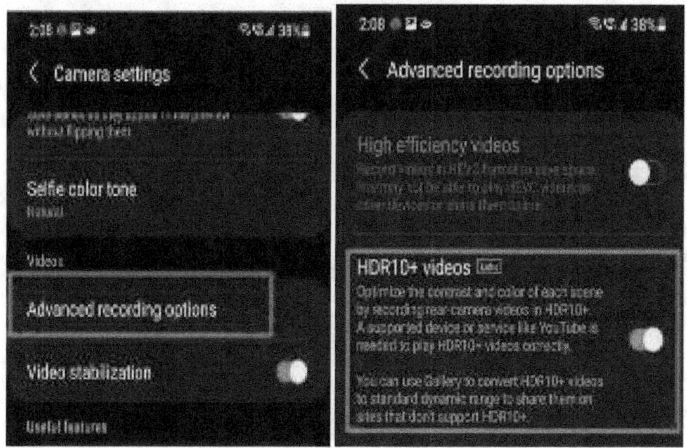

Capturing moving objects

This setting allows you to capture images of moving objects without much difficulty. To turn on this feature, do the following:

- Launch the camera app
- Go to camera settings
- Navigate down till you see **Tracking auto focus**
- **Turn on** the switch for Tracking auto focus

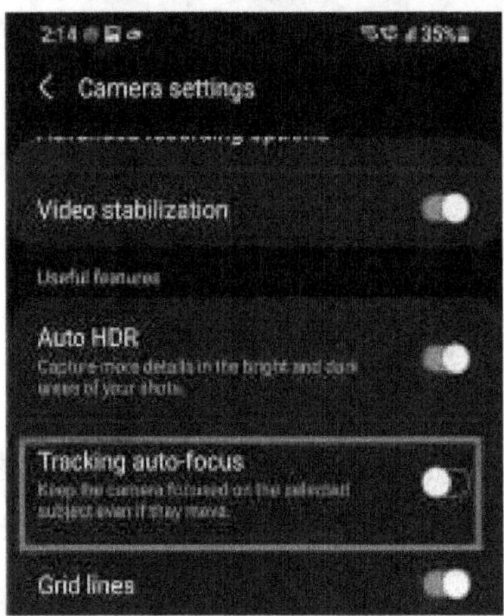

Changing selfie color tone

For selfies, your s21 allows you to choose from two color tones: Natural and Warm. In case you prefer to have a warm color tone for your images and videos, just follow steps outlined below:

- Launch the camera app and switch to **selfie mode**
- Next, go to **Settings** and navigate down till you view for Selfie color tone option
- **Tap on it** to specify your preferred color tone

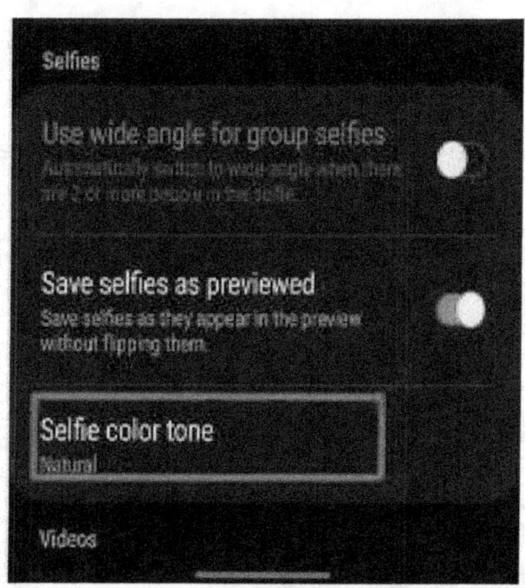

Deleting a picture(s), album(s) or video(s) from the gallery

- Go to the **gallery app**
- **Tap and hold** a picture, album or video to be deleted. If it's more than one, tick the others as well
- Next, tap **Delete** and confirm to delete the picture(s)
- Follow the same process for deleting an album(s)

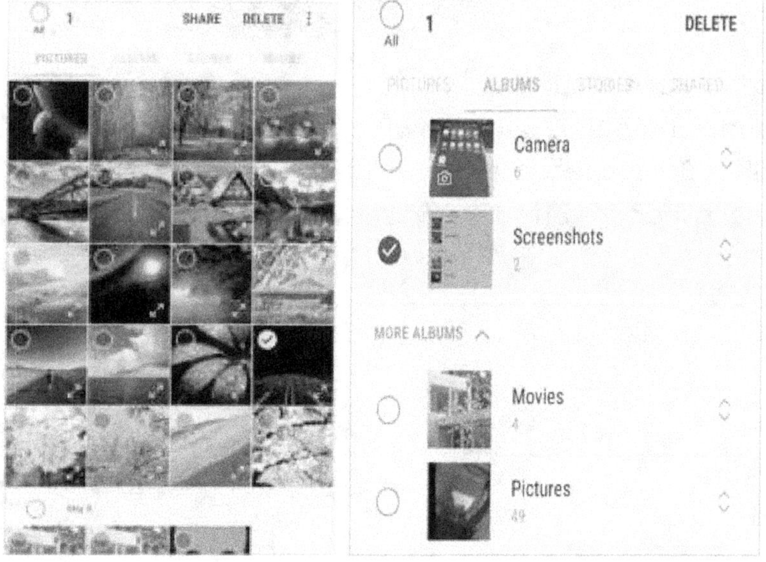

Chapter 10: screen shot and screen recording

Doing a screen shot

This function allows you to save and also share whatever you see on your screen just by pressing a combination of buttons. To do a screen shot, follow the steps below:

- Go to the screen where you want to take the screen shot
- Next, press the **volume down button** and the **side key** or power button simultaneously till the screen flashes
- To view the screen shot, go to the picture gallery of your device

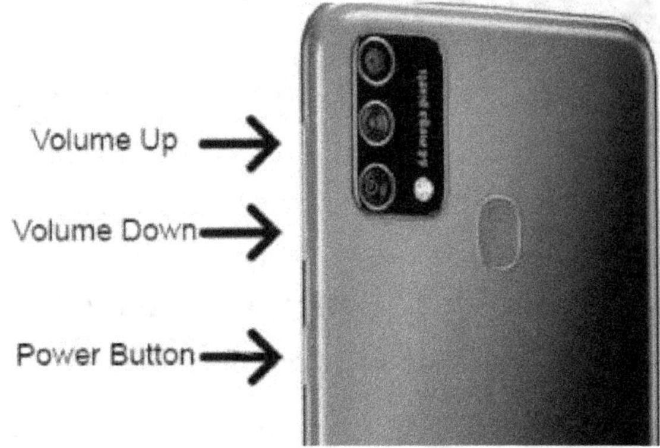

Doing a screen recording

- From screen top, **swipe down** to access the quick panel and select **Screen recorder**
- select your preferred sound setting and tap **Start recording**

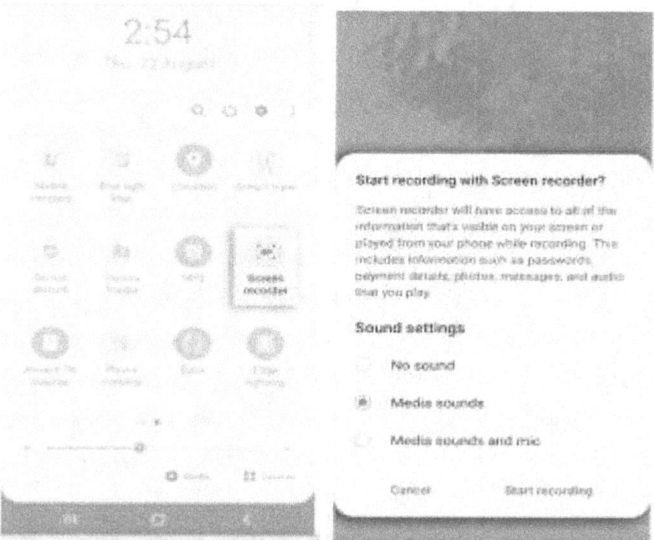

- From top right of the screen, you can choose between a range of options to add in your Screen Recording:

  1.   This allows you to write or draw on the screen

  2.   This will enable or disable the Picture-in-Picture feature (PiP) to record the screen with a video overlay of yourself.

  3.   When you are done recording the video, tap the Stop button

Screen recorder settings

If you aren't satisfied with the default settings of the screen recorder, you can alter them to suit your desire and preference. You can change a variety of settings such as sound and video quality and selfie video size. To change any of these settings, follow the guide below:

- From screen top, swipe down to launch the quick settings panel
- Tap **Screen recorder**
- Choose your desired sound and video quality and tap **Done** when you have chosen your preferred settings

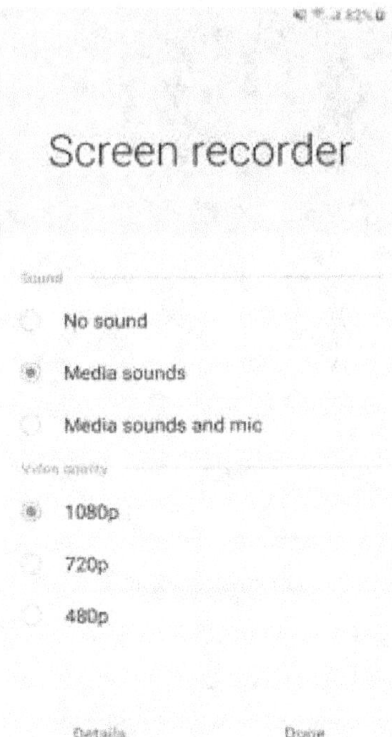

- To access the advanced settings, do the following:
  1. Launch **Settings**
  2. Go to **Advanced features**
  3. Tap **Screen shots and screen recorder**

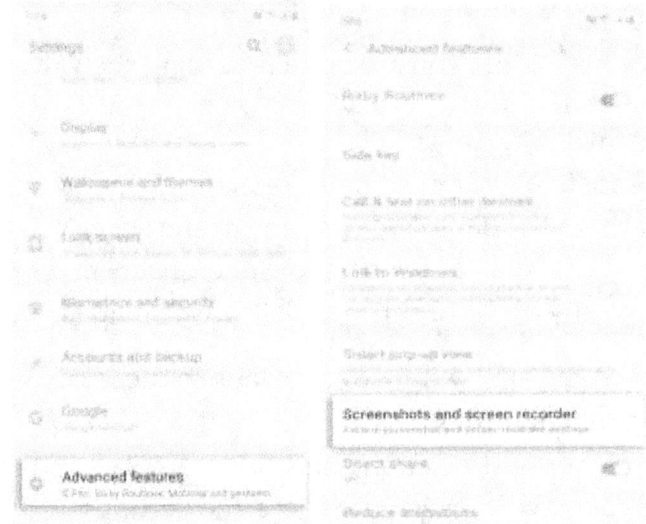

  4. Tap on **Screen recorder settings**

5. You can now change the **sound, video quality** and **selfie video size options** settings

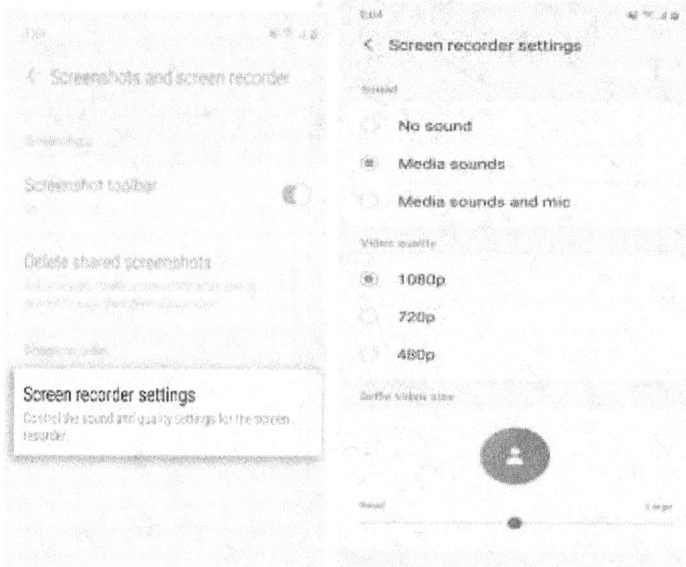

Deleting or sharing a screen shot

- Launch the **gallery** or **file manager** containing the screen shotted image
- To delete the image, **tap and hold** its icon and then tap **Delete**. Confirm the delete action. To delete more than one screen shot image, just tap and hold on one and then tick the others in like manner and tap **Delete** and confirm the action
- To share a screen shot, after taking the shot, select the option to send. Another way is to locate the image in the gallery or file manager that contains your screen shots, find the image, **tap and hold** it till you view the options. Select **Send** and then finish the process

Locating screen recordings in the My Files app

- Go to the **My Files app**
- Tap **Videos**

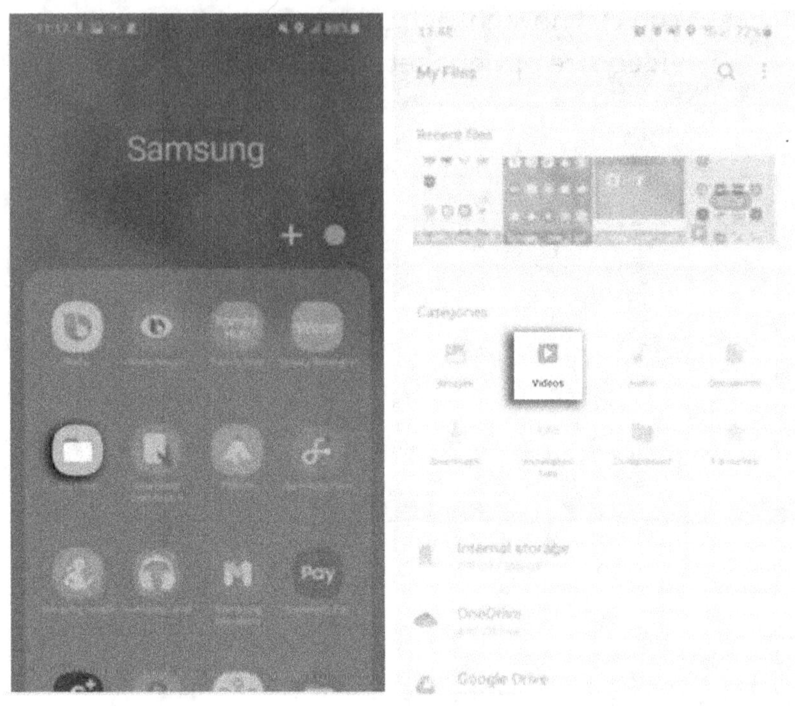

- Next, select **Screen recordings**
- You would now be able to view all saved screen recordings

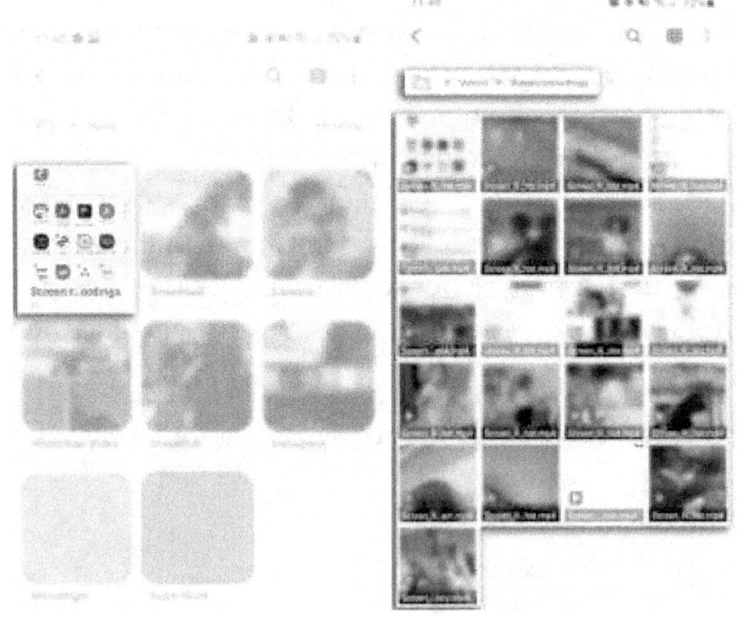

Chapter 11: Always on display

If you have ever wished that you could view stuff on your phone without having to press any button, then that wish has come true with the "Always on" display or AOD and its available on your S21. With the always on display, you can view your notifications, missed calls, time, date and more even if the screen is turned off. It doesn't end there because if you happen to have the one UI interface, there's actually a lot more you can do. Find how to use the AOD in this chapter.

Turning the always on display on or off

- Go to **Settings**
- Tap **Lock screen**
- Select **Always on Display**
- Use the switch to activate or deactivate it
- You can also access various settings of the **always on display** via this screen

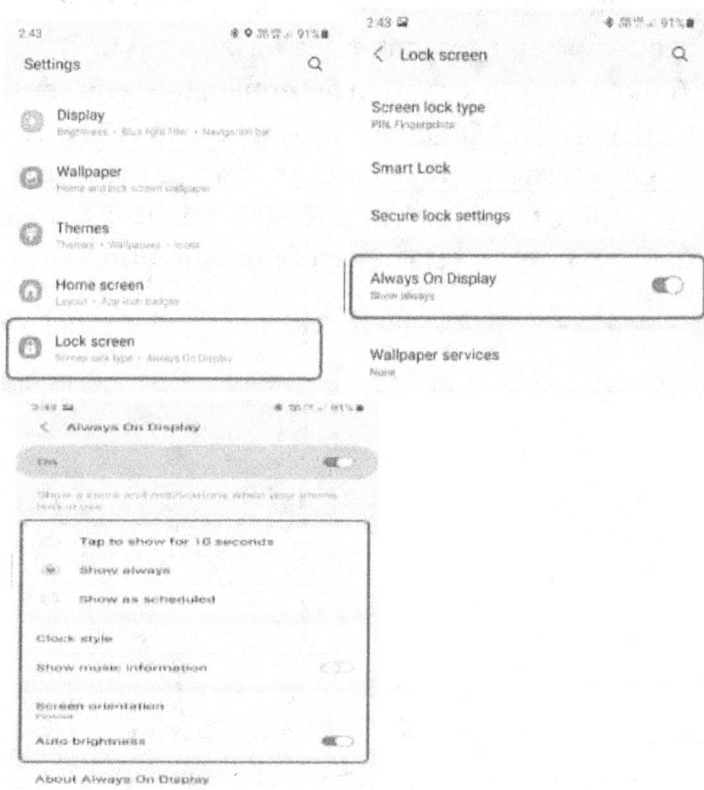

Adjusting the Always on Display options and settings

- Follow the first 3 steps as outlined above in how to turn the Always on display on or off
- When you get to the Always on display screen, the following options are available:
  1. You can decide if the AOD would only show for 10 seconds or indefinitely by staying on continuously. Select your preference by choosing **Tap to show for 10 seconds** or **show always**
  2. If you prefer to set the AOD to show at set times, tap **Show as scheduled**
  3. You can adjust the clock settings by changing the type and color
  4. Tap **Show music information** if you would prefer to view music data on your screen even when its off
  5. You can alternate the screen orientation between **Landscape** and **portrait** mode based on your choice
  6. You can allow the system determine the brightness setting of the AOD by allowing it to be on the **Auto bright** setting or you can set your preferred brightness by tapping the **switch** beside **Auto brightness** and then use the **slider** to set your preferred brightness level

Customizing the AOD clock style

- Go to **Settings,** locate and tap **Always on Display**
- Tap **Always on Display** again and select **Clock style**

- Choose your preferred clock style
- If you want to change the default color, tap **Color** and select a new color. Tap **Done** when you are ok

Chapter 12: Biometrics and security

Your S21 comes with a multi-level or layer security system to make sure that your device can't be accessed by unauthorized persons; and in the eventuality of theft, your data can't be easily accessed. These security features include face recognition, iris scanning and fingerprint scanning. Iris scanning is considered as the most secure authentication because it's not easy to get around. In the alternative, Face recognition and fingerprint scanning are faster and more convenient means of unlocking your device. No matter what security feature you decide to use on your phone, the steps to use in setting it up are outlined here.

Registering or adding a fingerprint

- First, set up a basic lock screen type which could be PIN, pattern or password based
- **Swipe upwards** from screen bottom to go to the app viewer display
- Tap **Settings**
- Navigate down to **Biometrics and security**
- Since you want to add or register a new fingerprint, tap **Fingerprints**

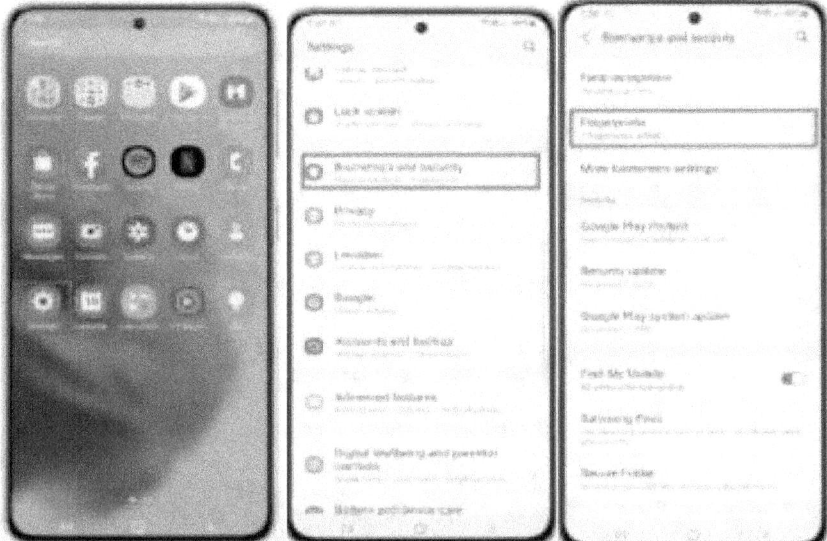

- If needed, enter your **passcode, pattern** or **PIN**

- Next, tap **Add fingerprint** to continue
- Next, place and press your finger on the red square with a fingerprint image at the center close to top of your screen
- Follow the on-screen directions till you get a confirmation that the fingerprint has been added
- Next, tap **Add** at bottom left of screen if you want to include another fingerprint or tap **Done** at bottom right if you don't want to

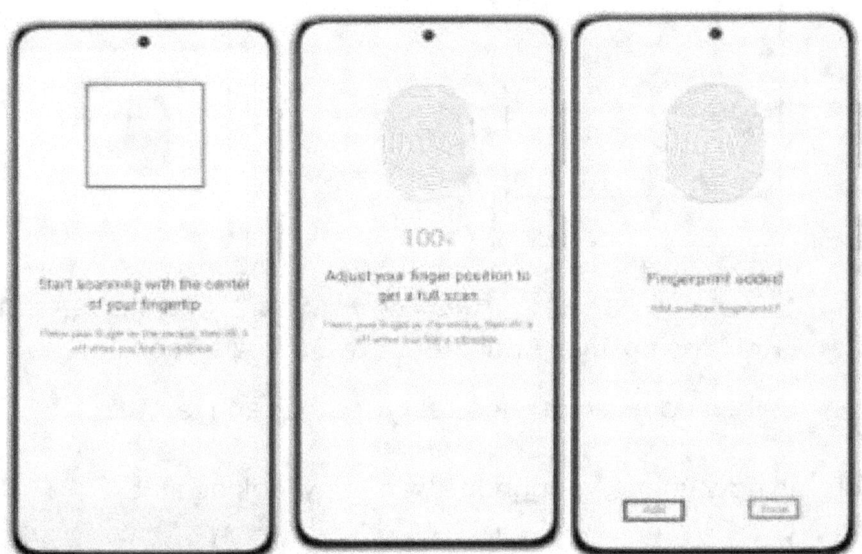

Setting up Face recognition

- You must have set up a screen lock either by a PIN, pattern or passcode
- Go to **Settings**
- Select **Biometrics and security**
- Tap **Face recognition**
- Confirm If you use glasses or not
- Tap **Continue**
- Next, hold the phone about 8-20 inches away from your face and place your face inside the circle

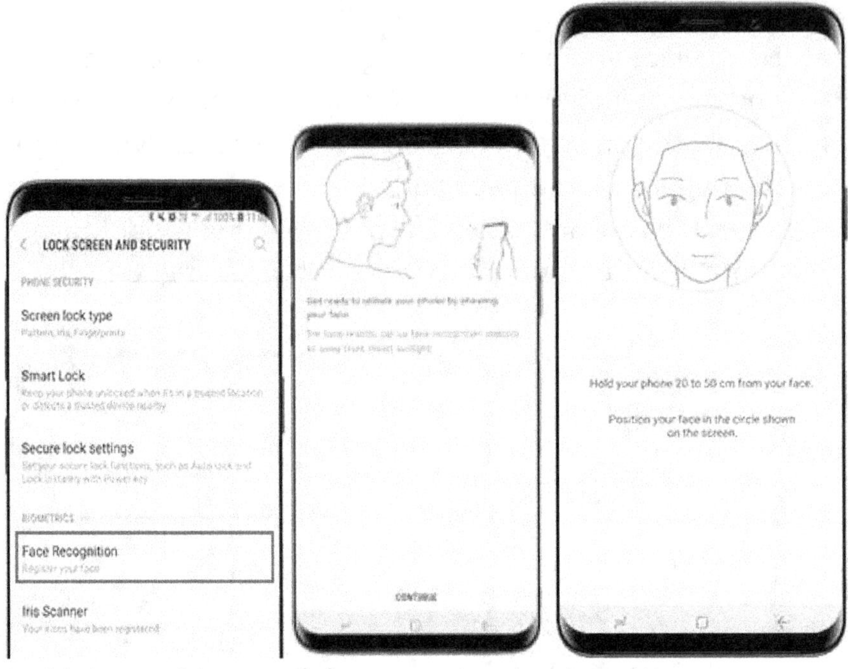

- Hold the position until the status bar reads 100%

- When done, adjust necessary settings and tap **OK**

You can now unlock your phone by merely looking at it.

Facial recognition options

There are additional security and settings options available to you after you have set up your device for face recognition as a means of unlocking and accessing your device. To view and alter these options, you have to go to **Settings,** go to **Biometrics and security** and then tap **Face recognition**. Once you do this, you can now manipulate the following options listed below:

- To delete any face data, tap **Remove face data**
- To make facial recognition more effective by including an alternate appearance, tap **Add alternative look**
- To unlock your phone using your face, tap **Face unlock**

- To keep the lock screen in view till you swipe the screen, tap **Stay on lock screen**
- To increase or enhance the recognition speed, tap **Faster recognition**
- To make open eyes a requirement for added security when using your face to unlock your phone**,** tap **Require open eyes**
- For added illumination in a dark place in order to aid the facial recognition system, tap **Brighten screen**
- For internet activity security use the facial recognition system by tapping **Samsung pass**

Samsung pass

This added security feature only works with Samsung internet and other supported apps. It makes it easier for you to sign into websites. With this feature, you needn't memorize passwords or IDs. It uses biometric data such as fingerprints or irises to grant you access and keep your accounts safe and secure.

Registration

- Launch **Settings**
- Go to **Biometrics and security**
- Navigate to **Samsung pass**, tap on it, tap **Agree** and enter your Samsung account information and tap **OK**

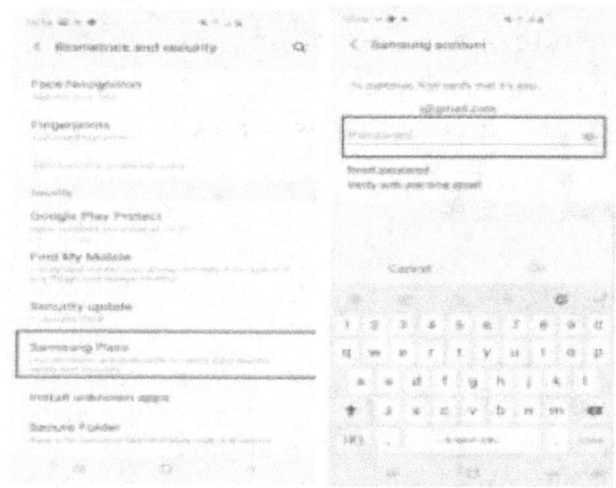

- Tap **Fingerprints** or **Irises** and follow the on-screen prompts to finish the process and tap **Done**

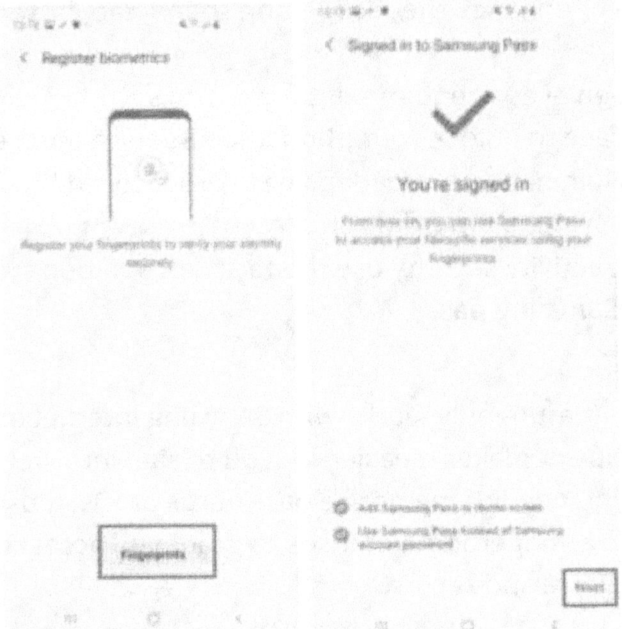

- Tap **Next** at screen bottom right to complete the process and start using Samsung pass

Using Samsung pass

When you register with Samsung pass, follow the steps below:

- Log into any website or app via Samsung internet
- You will get a message asking if you prefer to save your biometric information to make it easier for you to log into websites or apps

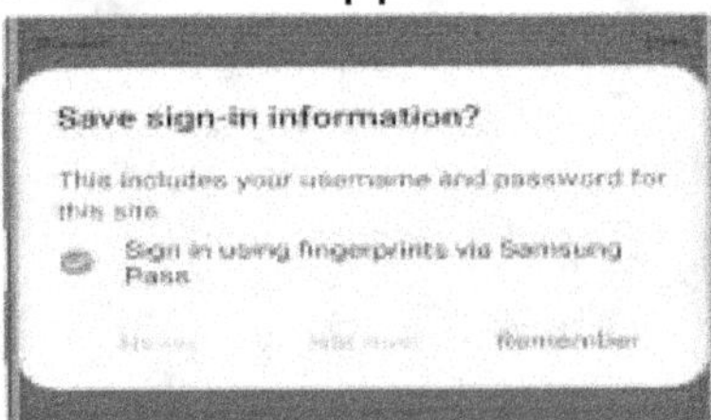

- If you agree or tap **Remember,** the next time you log into an app or website, all you need do is scan your fingerprint or Iris

Managing passwords and saved data

- Launch **Settings**
- Select **Biometrics and security**
- Tap **Samsung pass**
- Sign in to **Samsung pass** using your registered biometric method
- You would view a list of apps and websites you use Samsung pass with under the sign-in tab
- you can now tap on any of the apps or websites to view its login details and password
- you can view, edit or delete data for any of the apps or website

Deleting or editing saved data from Samsung pass

- **launch Settings**
- Go to **Biometrics and security**
- Tap **Samsung pass**

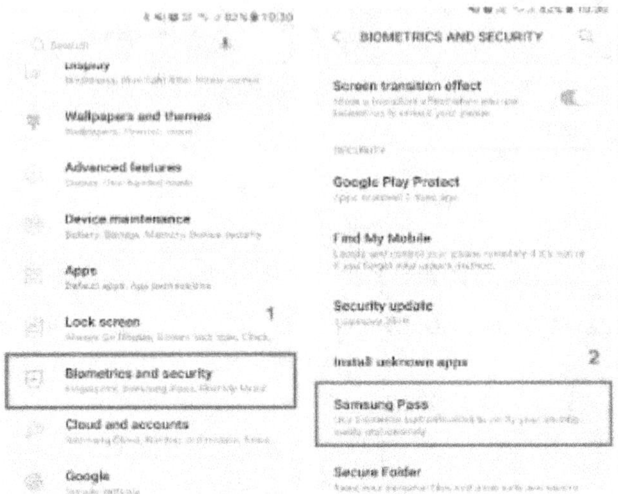

- Log in using your **biometric data**
- Tap on any **app** or **website**

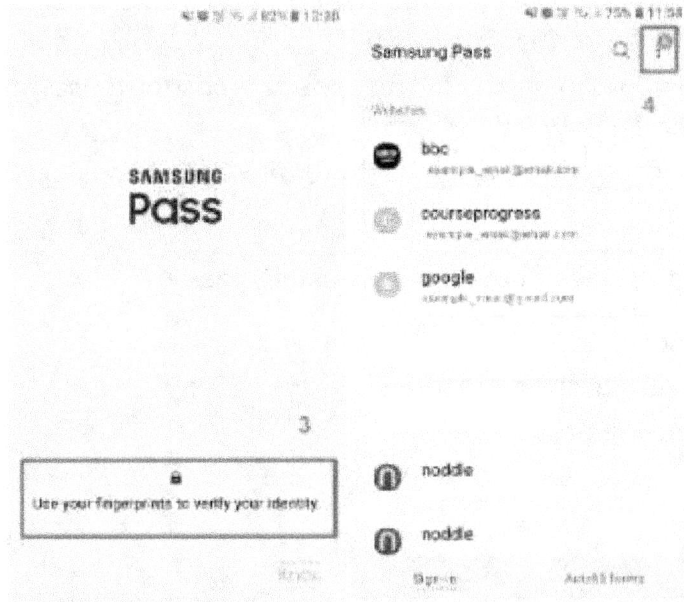

- You can edit or delete any data of your choice

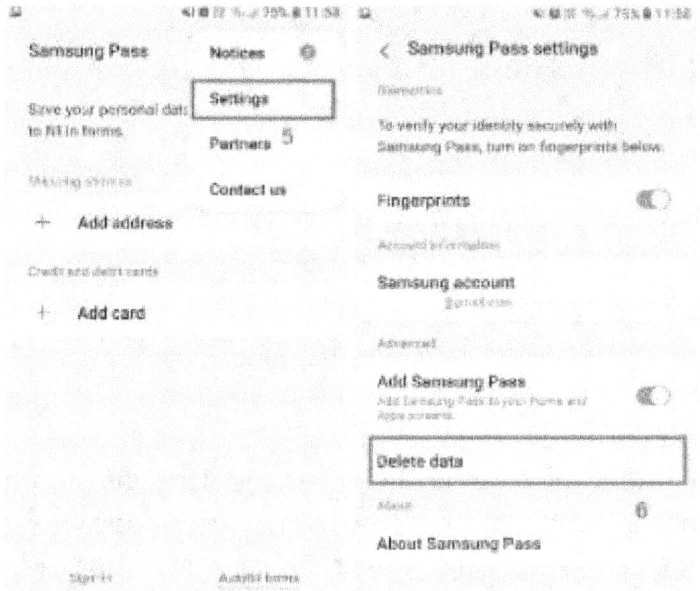

Turning Samsung pass off

- Launch **Settings**
- Go to **Biometrics and security**
- Tap **Samsung pass**
- Tap **More options** as represented by 3 vertical dots and tap **Settings**
- Next, tap **See all devices using Samsung pass** and tap **Remove** on the entry for your device
- When you tap on Remove on the popup, all data pertaining to Samsung pass would be wiped from your phone and Samsung pass would be reset
- Tap **OK** when done

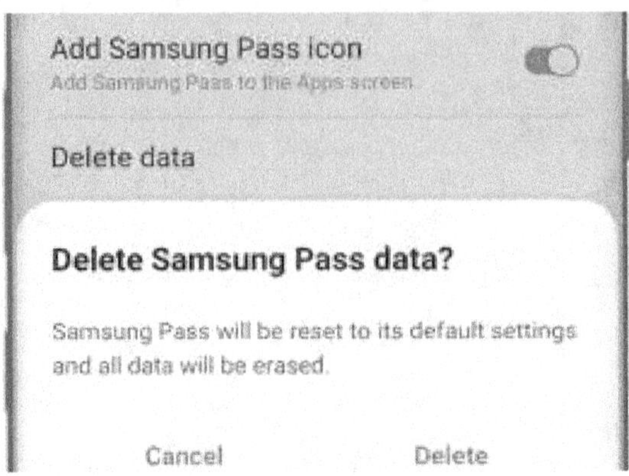

Creating a secure folder

Use the secure folder to store sensitive files and data on your phone. This folder enables you to create a private encrypted space on your device when you can store things you don't want unauthorized persons to view even if the phone is unlocked. You have the option of using a biometric or passcode security system to access the secure folder. To use this function, you must have signed into your Samsung account.

- **Swipe upwards** from home screen bottom to access apps display
- Tap **Settings**
- Go to **Biometrics and security**
- Navigate to the security section and tap **Secure folder**
- Tap **Agree** at screen bottom
- Next, if need be, choose your preferred identity authentication method
- Enter your Samsung password on the next display to continue

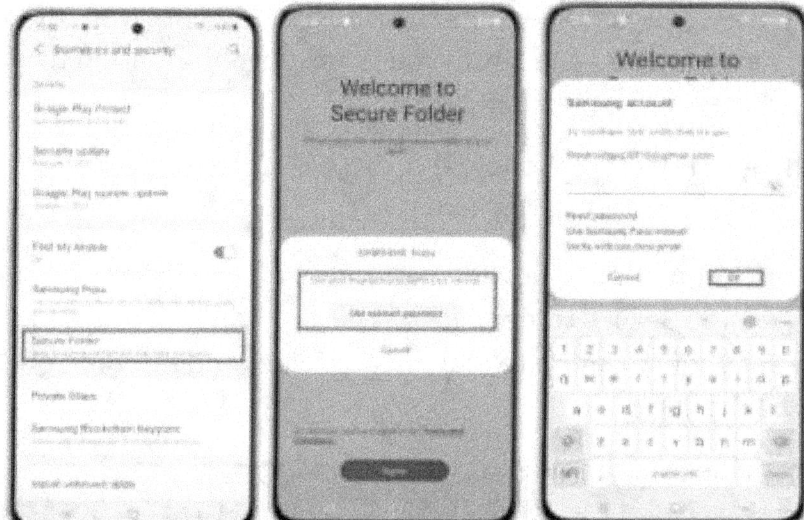

- Next, choose your preferred secure folder security lock type

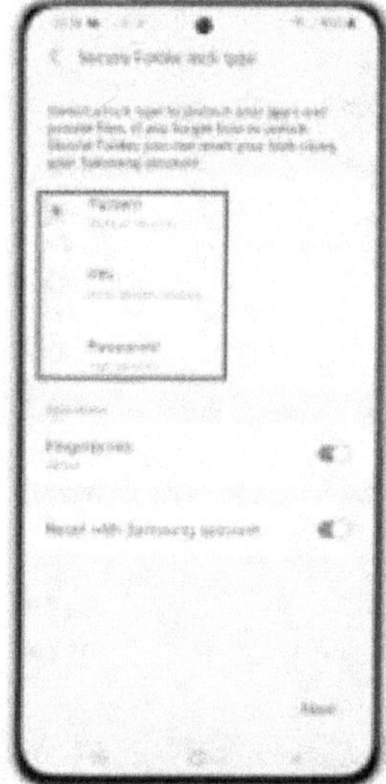

- You can now start storing your sensitive data including images, apps, contact details, events, documents etc in the folder
- To add new content in the folder, tap the +sign at upper right side of screen and follow screen prompts
- To lock and exit the folder, tap the triple dots beside the + sign and tap **Lock and exit** from the pop-up menu

- To access the folder, press its short cut symbol from the apps viewer display and key in your Samsung information to view the contents of the folder

Hiding or unhiding the folder

- Launch **Settings**
- Go to **Biometrics and security**
- Tap **Secure folder**
- Choose option to hide secure folder and tap **Hide** or **OK** to confirm

To access the secure folder, do the following:

- Launch **Settings**
- Tap **Biometrics and security**
- Tap **Secure folder** menu
- Tap **secure** folder symbol at screen bottom

Chapter 13: Near field communication technology and contactless payments

NFC technology is a means of effecting payment for goods or services, make secure transactions, exchange digital content and establish a connection between devices with just a touch. For NFC to work properly, both devices have to be close to each other. This due to the short-range nature of NFC transmissions. You can use NFC to make payments on the Samsung pay platform. To set up NFC on your phone, do the following:

Activating NFC

- Launch **Settings**
- Tap **Connections**
- Next, tap **NFC and contactless payments**

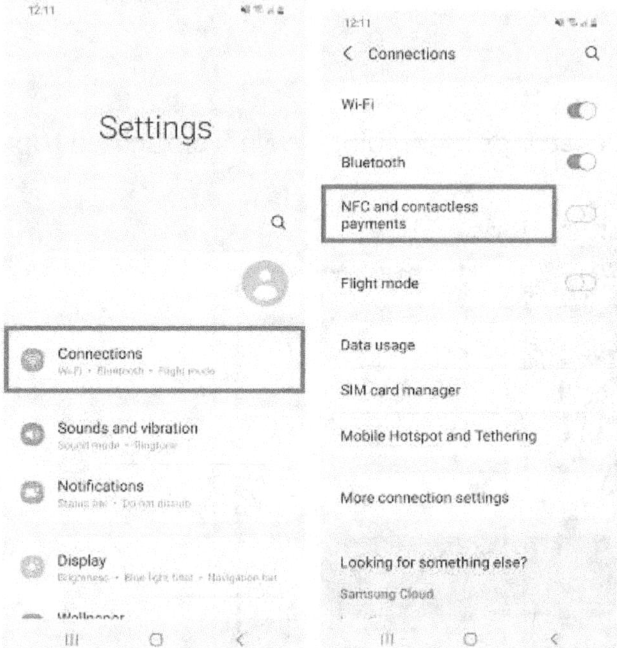

- On the next display, activate NFC by turning the **switch** on
- Tap **Contactless payments**
- Next, choose your preferred mobile payment service and follow the instructions to finish the set-up

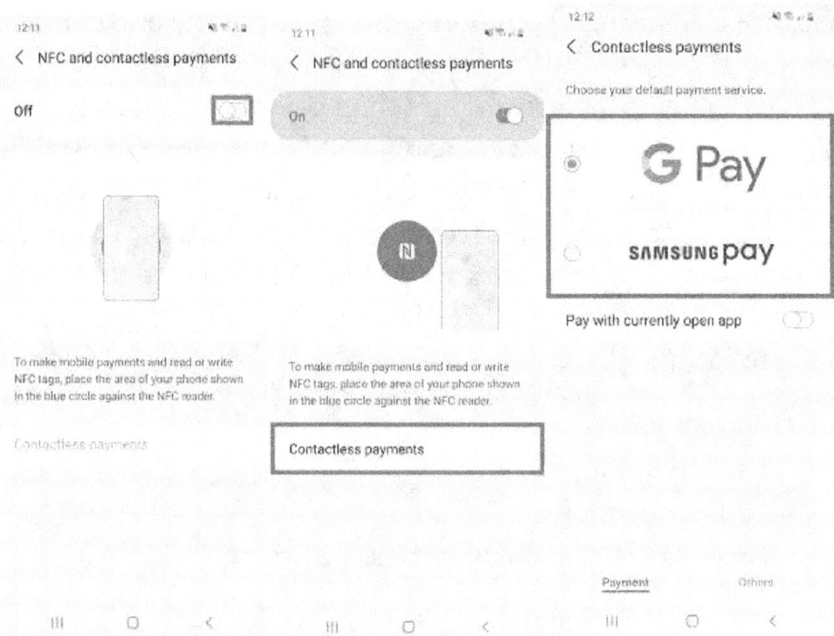

Turning NFC on or off

- Launch **quick settings** by swiping down from screen top
- Tap **Settings**
- Next, tap **Connections**

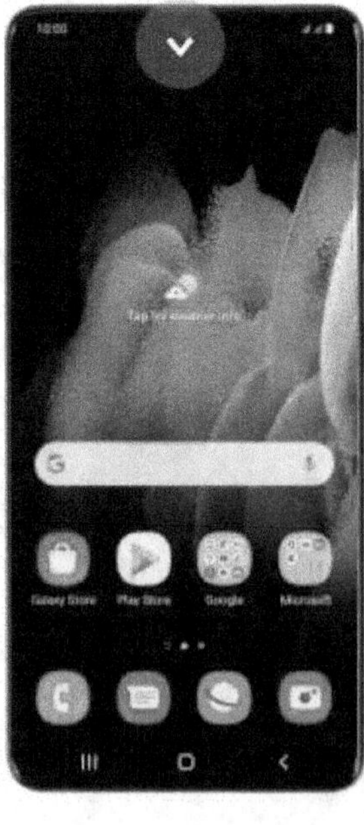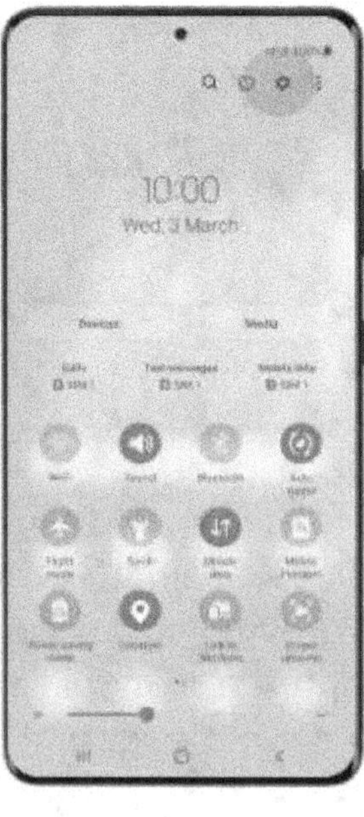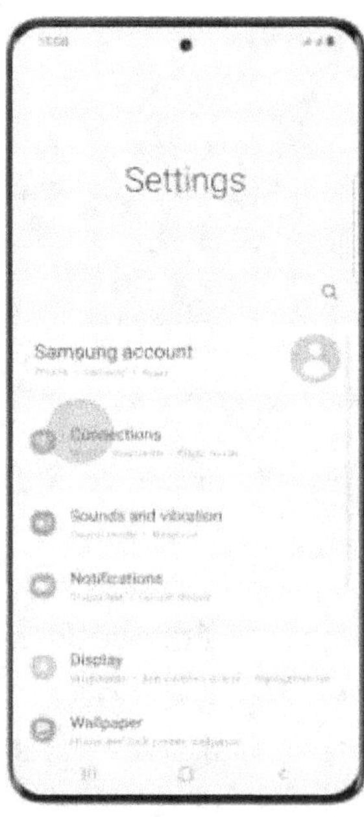

- Tap **NFC and contactless payments**
- Use the **switch** to turn NFC on or off

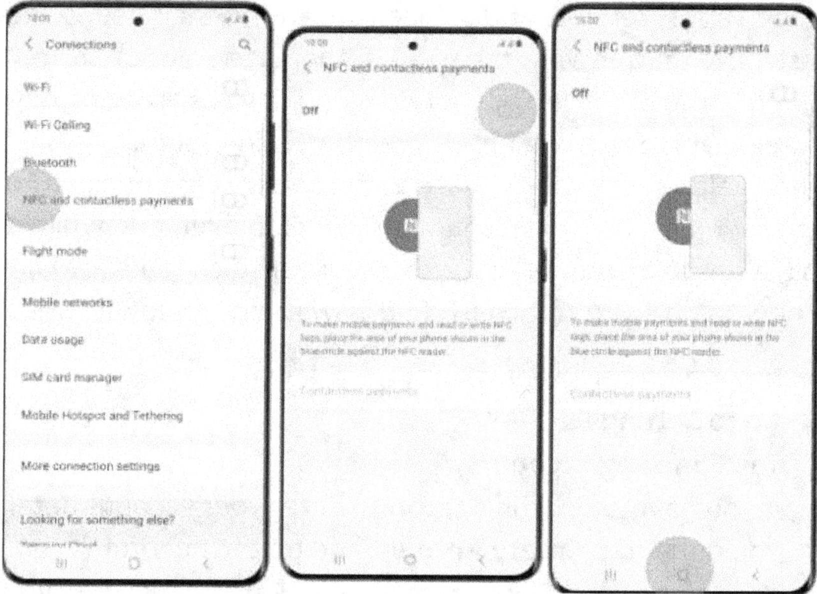

Chapter 14: Samsung apps, devices and services

For those who are loyal to the Samsung brand, the manufacturer has developed apps, services and devices to cater to their needs and make life easier. No matter what the need is, there is a solution from Samsung. Some of these apps services and devices are Samsung pay, Samsung health, Samsung notes, members, kids, global goals, galaxy shop and galaxy wearable. To access these services and apps you may have to set up a Samsung account. If you didn't set it up while doing the initial set up of your phone, you can refer to chapter 7 (Mail) to learn how to do so. You can also find how to do it below:

Setting up a Samsung account

- Go to **Settings**
- Tap **Samsung accounts**
- If you have an existing account, enter your account details. If you don't, tap **Create Account** and do the needful
- You can also tap **Reset password** or **Find ID** based on your intentions

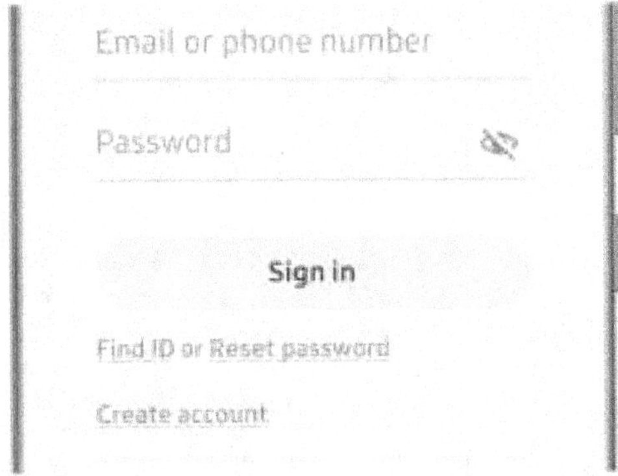

Setting up and using Samsung pay

Samsung pay is an offering from Samsung that gives users the option or ability to make contactless payments with their phone

- Launch **Samsung pay** from the app drawer
- Sign in to your Samsung account if necessary
- Tap **Get started**

- Set up a PIN different from your lock screen PIN
- Confirm the PIN
- Next, follow the directions to add payment cards
- Tap **Samsung Pay Home** when done

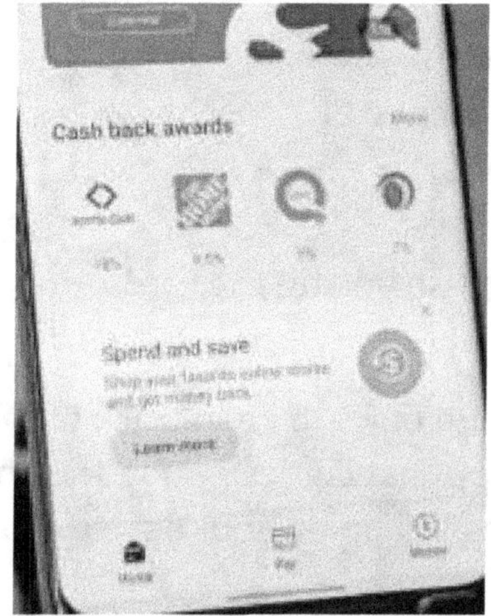

Using Samsung pay to make payments

- From bottom of home screen, **swipe upwards**
- Choose the required debit or credit card. Swipe left or right to find required card if not in view
- Tap the PIN button at screen bottom below your card tap the finger print sensor in case you are using that security option
- To make the payment, place the back of the phone near the payment terminal or card machine
- If required, enter the card PIN

Adding a card

You can add upwards of 10 credit or debit cards on the Samsung payment platform. To add more, follow the steps below:

- Launch the **Samsung pay** app
- Tap the **menu button** at top left
- Next, tap **Cards**
- Choose **Add Card** from the menu
- Tap **Add credit/debit card**
- Follow screen instructions to finish adding the card

Samsung Health

Samsung has made it possible for health buffs to keep track of their health data and activity via a health app that comes preloaded on the phone. (in case you don't have the health app on your device, you can download it from the play store).

- Launch the **Samsung health app** and preview the information
- Decide if you would like to get marketing information and tap **Agree**
- Next, allow the necessary permissions
- If you are logged in to an existing Samsung account, you would be asked if you want to sync your data
- If you are not logged in to an account, you would have to sign in before you can access the health app. To do so, tap **Sign in** and enter your details
- If you don't have a Samsung account yet, tap **Sign in** and then tap **Create new account** and follow the on-screen directions

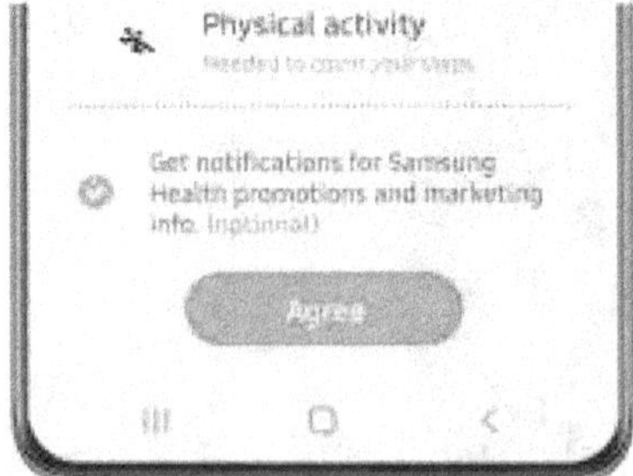

Managing personal information on the health app

- Launch the **Samsung health app**
- Tap the **menu** symbol as shown by 3 horizontal lines
- Next, tap **Profile**
- From here, you can adjust your personal information such as name, picture, height, weight, etc

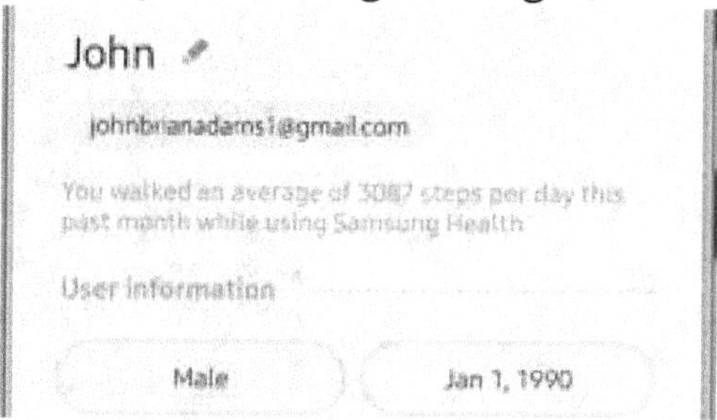

Setting up Samsung kids

Samsung has created a kids friendly package and also made it easy for parents to control their kids digital activities simply by setting controls and limits to make sure that their kids aren't exposed to inappropriate content while allowing them access to harmless, educative and fun apps and sites.

- Launch the **quick access panel** by **swiping down** from screen top
- Locate and tap **Samsung kids** on the **quick access panel**
- Tap **Next** on the Samsung kids welcome page

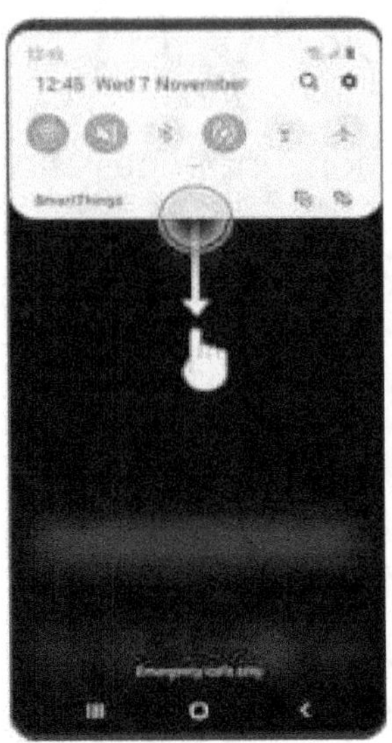 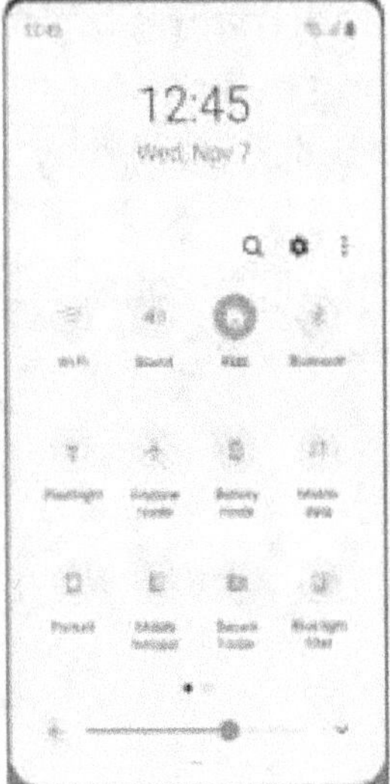 

- Set up a **PIN** and confirm it in order to be able to access Samsung kids

- Tap the **menu button** at top right to set limits on daily playtime, apps, sites and contacts your kids can access and that's all that there is to it.

Pairing and using a Galaxy wearable device to your S21

The Galaxy Wearable app connects your wearable devices to your mobile phone. It also manages and monitors the wearable device features and apps you have installed through Galaxy Apps. To connect a galaxy wearable to your mobile phone, you have to install the Samsung galaxy wearable app on it. You can get the app from Galaxy Apps. To pair a Galaxy wearable to your phone, follow the steps below:

- Activate your Bluetooth on your phone and turn on your galaxy wearable
- You may be asked to pair the device via your home screen. if this happens, tap **Add now.** If it doesn't show on your home screen, you may have to launch the Galaxy wearable app and select the wearable from therein
- Next, tap on the device model

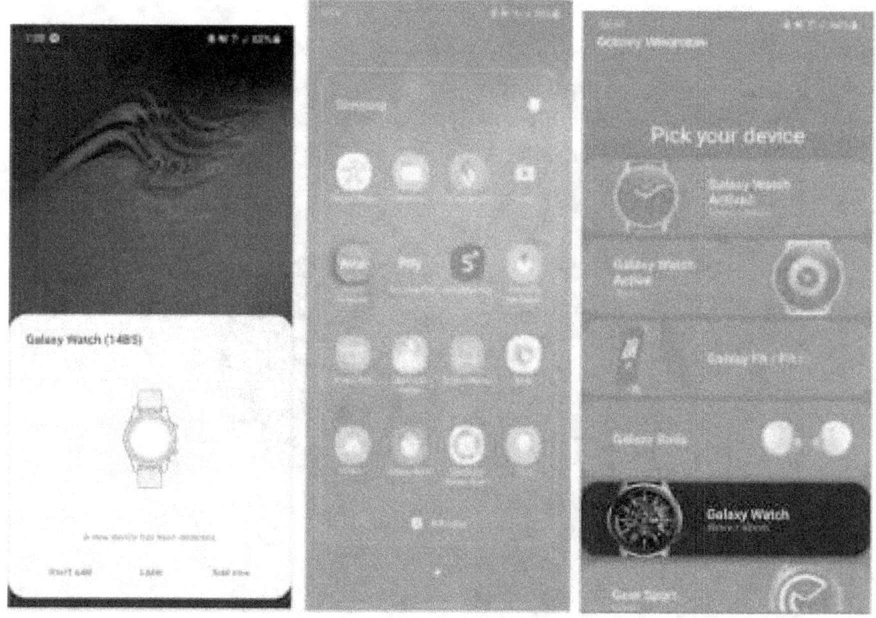

- Tap **OK** on your phone and the wearable to pair both devices

- Let both devices finish pairing

- Agree to the **Privacy Policy** and **User License Agreement**

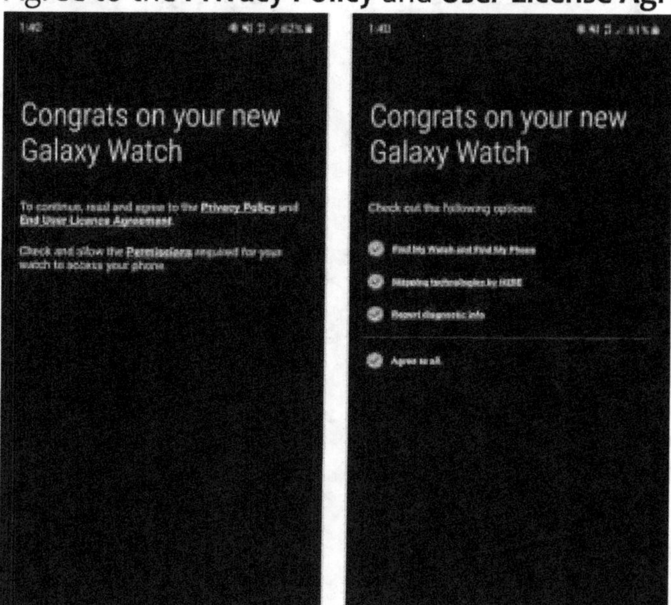

- Select if you would prefer to **Locate a backup** or **Skip for now** and tap **Next.** This marks the conclusion of the pairing process

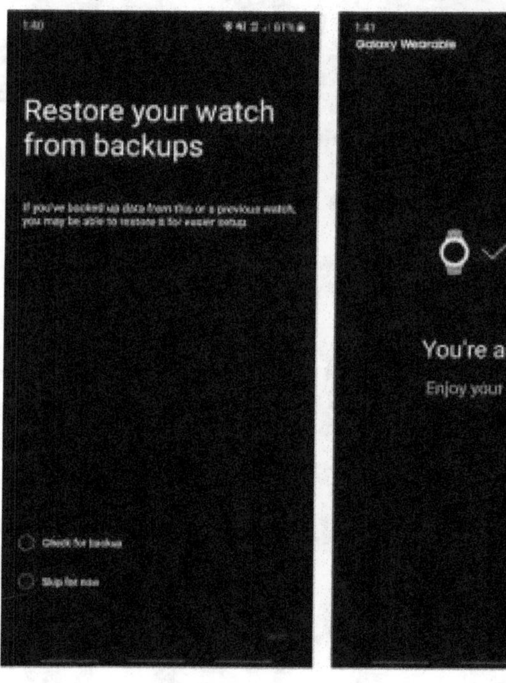

- You would now be able to view your connected wearable via the **Galaxy wearable app**

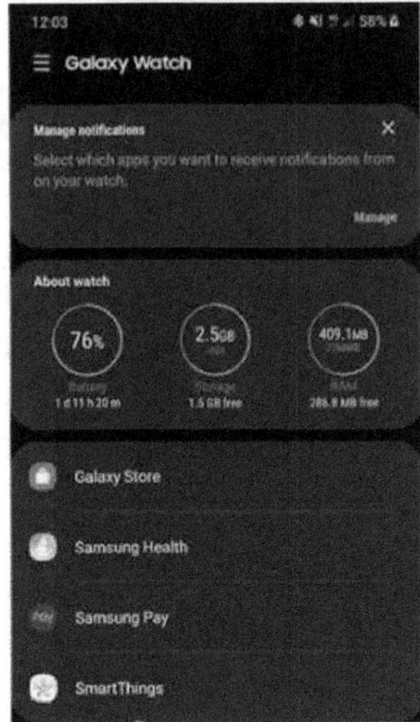